PUFFIN BOOKS

THE PUFFIN DICTIONARY OF COMPUTER WORDS

Computer jargon can be amazing – sometimes it sounds like English, sometimes it sounds like a language from outer space. And it is used everywhere – in school, at home, in magazines and on radio and television. But what does it all mean?

Here is a clear, concise and wonderfully illustrated dictionary with many of the answers you will need. Each word is given a detailed definition and is explained in a lively way, using everyday examples to help make the meaning clear.

From Alphanumeric to Zero suppression, from the simplicity of the Abacus to the intricacies of VisiCalc®, this new and exciting dictionary defines more than 400 words and phrases – making a perfect reference book for everyone learning about computers.

Illustrated by Jack Freas

Robert W. Bly

THE PUFFIN DICTIONARY OF
COMPUTER WORDS

Puffin Books

Puffin Books, Penguin Books Ltd, Harmondsworth, Middlesex, England
Viking Penguin Inc., 40 West 23rd Street, New York, New York 10010, U.S.A.
Penguin Books Australia Ltd, Ringwood, Victoria, Australia
Penguin Books Canada Ltd, 2801 John Street, Markham, Ontario, Canada L3R 1B4
Penguin Books (N.Z.) Ltd, 182–190 Wairau Road, Auckland 10, New Zealand

First published in the U.S.A. as *A Dictionary of Computer Words* by Banbury Books, Inc. 1983
This revised edition first published in Puffin Books 1984

Copyright © Robert W. Bly, 1983
All rights reserved

Typeset, printed and bound in Great Britain by
Hazell Watson & Viney Limited
Member of the BPCC Group
Aylesbury, Bucks
Set in 10/12pt VIP Univers Light

Except in the United States of America, this book is sold subject
to the condition that it shall not, by way of trade or otherwise, be lent,
re-sold, hired out, or otherwise circulated without the
publisher's prior consent in any form of binding or cover other than
that in which it is published and without a similar condition
including this condition being imposed on the subsequent purchaser

To Gary Blake – friend, teacher and colleague

ACKNOWLEDGEMENTS

I'd like to thank Eric Marks for shaping the concept and content of this work; my fiancée Amy Sprecher for enduring the neglect that preparing this book necessitated; and my former supervisors at Westinghouse, Terry C. Smith and Tom Quirk, for teaching me a thing or two about writing.

INTRODUCTION

If you want to learn a foreign language, it helps to have a dictionary by your side. Otherwise, you might have trouble making sense of the many strange and unfamiliar words you encounter in your study of the language, whether you're a student of French, Spanish, Russian – or even computer language.

By computer language, we don't mean the special codes computer programmers use to communicate with their machines. We mean the jargon, slang words and other made-up terms computer people use to talk to each other.

Professionals in any field – computers, construction, economics, insurance – invent special terms to describe their activities. Within the profession, these terms are a useful shorthand. But they also make the goings-on of the profession a mystery to outsiders. And as more and more slang is invented, ordinary people need a translator to understand what the technical people are saying.

This dictionary is written to be your translator and guide to the jargon of computer technology.

Computer jargon comes in many varieties. Sometimes, a familiar object is given a new, more complicated name (computer people call television screens *video monitors*). In other cases, familiar words take on new meanings. To us, a ram is a sheep. But in computer jargon, *RAM* stands for *random access memory*, a place within the computer that holds the instructions the machine is to perform and the data it is to work on.

Some computer lingo sounds like proper scientific terminology – *hardware, software, operating system, parity check*. But other computer terms sound as if they come from the vocabulary of a Martian – *glitch, kludge, MOS, GIGO*. And a few computer phrases sound downright sinister: to *crash* the system, to operate in a *crippled mode*, to be caught in a *deadly embrace*.

The Puffin Dictionary of Computer Words is a concise guide to computer terms, written for beginners who need a quick introduction to the field and for people who use computers but want to know more about what the jargon means. You don't need any special background or knowledge of computers to use this book – anyone can pick it up, read it, enjoy it and learn from it.

The book contains more than 400 entries. In every case, we have tried to define the terms using plain, simple English. Some computer words, however, must be defined in terms of other computer words. So if a word is new to you, it's probably defined elsewhere in the dictionary.

The computer field is one of the five fastest-growing industries of the decade. There are already approaching 2½ million home computers in Britain, more per head of population than in any country in the world, and in 1983 alone 1·4 million of these machines were sold.

The computer industry changes rapidly, and with every technical innovation come dozens of new buzz words. We believe *The Puffin Dictionary of Computer Words* is the clearest, most accurate, most up-to-date dictionary of computer terms in print. But, if you think we've omitted an important term or included a definition that isn't clear, please write and let us know. Because of all the mail we receive, we won't be able to respond with a personal letter. But you will have our thanks for helping us to keep up with the constantly expanding vocabulary of computer technology.

– Robert W. Bly
New York City

Abacus A hand-held counting device that consists of beads strung on a series of wooden rods. The user moves the beads to count, add, subtract, multiply and divide. The abacus was invented by the Chinese more than 2,000 years ago.

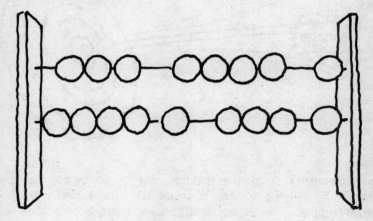

Access The process of obtaining information from the memory, terminal or some other part of a computer system. *To access data* means to retrieve information from a computer.

Access time The amount of time it takes for a computer to obtain information from a device such as a magnetic disk.

Accumulator The computer register where mathematical operations such as addition, subtraction, division and multiplication take place. The accumulator stores a number, receives another number, and then holds the result of any mathematical operation carried out on those two numbers. In this way the accumulator accumulates the results of the maths a computer does.

Accuracy How close an answer is to what it would be if it were perfect. Surprisingly, computers sometimes make very small mistakes in the arithmetic they do, and although this usually does not affect you there are occasions when it can. For instance, the correct answer to a sum might be 5, but the computer has worked it out as 5·00000001. If you ask in your program, 'Is the answer 5?' the machine will reply 'No', and your program will go wrong. You need to know how accurate your computer is — that is, how large its mistakes can be — and make allowances for that.

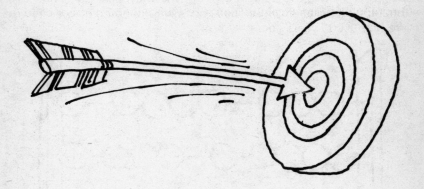

Acoustic coupler A modem that does not need to be connected with wires to the telephone line. You just take the ordinary telephone receiver and place it in the acoustic coupler. The coupler makes noises that the telephone picks up and sends down the line.

A/D Stands for Analog-to-Digital. To digest information from the real world, computers must convert physical information to a form that the computer can understand. An A/D converter is the device that accomplishes this. It changes information from analog, or continuous signals, to discrete, separate pieces of information — a form known as digital. (See also *analog* and *digital*.)

Ada A high-level programming language for real-time applications such as weapons systems. Named after Ada, Countess Lovelace, who was Charles Babbage's assistant.

Address You know that your address is a number (and a street name) that identifies the place where you live. The address signifies a specific location in your town, city or district.

In computers, the address refers to a specific location in the computer's memory. Each location in memory contains a different piece of information — just as a different family lives in each house in your street. A computer programmer uses the address to locate a particular piece of information he may need to run his program. For convenience, each location in a computer's memory is numbered consecutively.

A computer address can be identified with either a number code or letters of the alphabet, depending on whether you are using machine language or a high-level language.

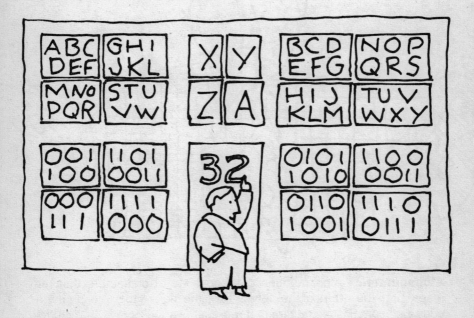

ALGOL A popular computer programming language used for solving mathematical and numerical problems. The language was named ALGOL because it was originally designed for solving algorithms — procedures for formulating and solving problems in logic and maths.

Algorithm A plan for solving a problem. Algorithms consist of a sequence of well-defined steps. All computer programs are algorithms.

An algorithm for selecting the right tie to wear might have the following steps:
1. Pick a tie from the rack.
2. Hold it against your shirt.
3. If the colours match, wear the tie.
4. If the colours do not match, replace the tie and go back to step #1.
5. If none of the ties match, go out and buy one that does.

Alphanumeric Alphanumeric code consists of characters that represent both the letters of the alphabet and the digits 0 to 9. Alphanumeric code also contains characters that represent various symbols, including punctuation marks and the signs for mathematical operations. Computer output may be represented as alphanumeric data (equations, symbols and sentences), or as graphic data (pictures, graphs and charts).

Analog In nature, physical quantities — temperature, light, heat, sound, pressure, distance — vary gradually. Thermometers, for example, show that temperature rises continuously; the mercury does not suddenly jump from 65°F to 78°F, skipping the values in between. Another example of analog can be found at the entrances to many buildings: ramps are continuous (analog); steps are not.

If an electric current is to measure and represent a physical quantity, it too must be continuous. *Analog signals* are electric signals that have a continuous range of voltages or currents.

Analog computer Analog computers handle numbers by representing them as voltages (or, less frequently, as some other continuously variable quantity such as fluid pressure, light or temperature). Analog computers consist of special amplifiers connected with wires and plugs. The main advantage of analog computers is that they can handle complex signals using simple, inexpensive circuitry. However, they have pretty much been replaced by digital computers.

AND A logical operation that compares information ('bits') in the computer.

A bit can be either a 1 or a 0. The result of the AND operation is 1 only if both of the bits being compared are 1.

'Words' in the computer are made up of many bits. The AND operation compares two words bit by bit.

Think of the AND operation using the example of two statements (A and B) and a conclusion (C). The conclusion is true only if both statements, A AND B, are also true:

Statement A – 'Computers can multiply faster than humans can.'
Statement B – 'I will do my homework tonight using a computer.'

If it is true that computers are faster than people and if it is also true that you are using a computer, then the conclusion C is true:

Conclusion C – 'I will be able to do the maths homework faster than the people in my class who do not use a computer.'

If, say, statement B is false – that is, if you do *not* do your homework on the computer – then the conclusion, C, is also false. That is how an AND operation works.

An *AND gate* is an electronic circuit whose output is 1 only if all of the inputs are 1.

APL A programming language for interactive terminals – the type of terminal where the user asks questions that are immediately answered by the computer. APL offers programmers many powerful mathematical functions, each represented by a special character. This concise notation makes programs written in APL shorter than programs written in other languages such as Pascal, BASIC and FORTRAN. APL is especially useful for handling arrays.

Applications package A program or set of programs written by the user to perform a specific task. Applications programs can balance savings accounts, keep track of airline reservations, solve trigonometry problems, and do all sorts of other useful work for people in school, business, government and industry.

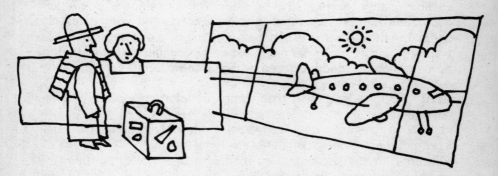

Architecture   To us, architecture is the design and construction of buildings. The goal of architecture is to produce a building that satisfies people's needs in terms of appearance, style and function.

To computer people, the term architecture refers to the design of a computer system. The goal of computer architecture is to organize the computer's components — processing units, memory, terminals, programs, etc. — in a way in which the different parts work together to achieve the objective of the design. Some computers, for example, may be designed to handle complex scientific calculations. Others may be constructed to perform boring, routine computations over and over again at very high speed.

Archived file   An archive is a place where records are stored. Some of the records may be quite old, and the term archive conjures up images of dusty, yellowing papers stuffed away in cartons, cabinets and shelves.

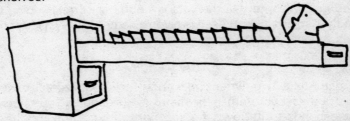

Because an archived file contains information that is not current, there's no need to be able to get to it quickly. And people will rarely look for it. In the computer, an archived file is not stored in the main memory within the computer itself. Instead, it is kept outside the computer on some secondary storage medium: magnetic tape, microfilm, disks . . . perhaps even on paper ('hard copy'). It is true that it takes longer to find, or access, information from secondary storage media, but in the case of archival information, speed is not of the essence.

Arithmetic instruction   An instruction that tells the computer to perform an arithmetic operation such as addition, subtraction, multiplication or division. These operations are performed upon numbers or variables called operands and yield a numerical result. For example, in the equation $3+2=5$, addition (+) is the arithmetic instruction, 3 and 2 are the operands, and 5 is the result.

Array A way of organizing pieces of information. There are two types of arrays: the vector and the matrix.

The vector is a one-dimensional array, a list of items in a horizontal row. You give each item in the vector a number corresponding to its place in the list, and the list itself is given a name, usually a letter of the alphabet. A vector named 'A' might look like this:

$$A_1 \; A_2 \; A_3 \; A_4 \; A_5 \; A_6 \; A_7 \ldots$$

The matrix is a two-dimensional array: it has horizontal rows and vertical columns. Each item in the matrix is assigned two numbers. The first corresponds to its row; the second, to its column. So, an item labelled B_{23} would be located in the second row and the third column of a matrix named 'B'. This matrix might look like this:

$$\begin{matrix} B_{11} & B_{12} & B_{13} \\ B_{21} & B_{22} & B_{23} \\ B_{31} & B_{32} & B_{33} \end{matrix}$$

Many computer languages have special instructions for creating and manipulating arrays. And some languages use arrays that are three-dimensional . . . four-dimensional . . . and higher!

Artificial intelligence The most advanced area of research in computing, in which scientists try to build computers that can see, hear, talk, and think to some degree as well as humans can. This work is very difficult and the scientists still have a long way to go. Their greatest success so far has been in the field of *expert systems*. (See also *robot* and *Turing test*.)

ASCII Stands for American Standard Code for Information Interchange. Pronounced 'ask-key'. A standard code by which computers convert the symbols on keyboards — letters, numbers, and characters such as full stops, plus signs and parentheses — into the numerical binary code that the machine can understand. Each keyboard character is represented by seven 'bits' (binary digits).

Assembly language Computers 'speak' and 'think' in a numerical code called machine language. But because people speak in words, it is difficult for us to read and write programs in this language — even though it's what the computer would prefer.

And so computer programmers invented assembly language, a simple language that replaces the numerical codes of machine language with easily remembered phrases that people can understand. Instead of writing '01100110' to tell the computer to begin its work, assembly language would let you write a word like 'LOAD' to do it.

A special computer program called an *assembler* automatically translates assembly language into machine language.

Even though assembly language is a big improvement over machine language, programming in assembly language is still a long, involved, error-prone process. That's why most people prefer to use an even simpler system of communication called high-level programming language.

Assignment statement The assignment statement, symbolized by the equal sign (=), lets you assign a numerical value to a variable. The assignment statement 'X = 5' means the variable 'X' is given a value of 5.

Asynchronous There are two ways in which computers can send information to each other. In one way (synchronous) the sending computer must transmit the information down the wire at exactly the time that the receiving machine is expecting it. In asynchronous working, the sending machine can transmit whenever it likes. This is simpler but not as fast as synchronous working.

Audit trail In any computer system, hundreds of thousands of different events take place each day — and sometimes each hour! Calculations are made, messages are exchanged, old information is taken out of storage, new information is recorded into memory.

An audit trail is a record of a specific transaction that takes place in the system. The trail is stored as a file (collection of information) and is created during routine processing of information.

Audit trails let you keep track of what is going on within the system. For example, if you use the computer to send messages to other computers, an audit trail provides a record of when the messages were sent, to whom they were sent and whether they were received. It's a handy tool for people who manage large data processing systems.

Automatic cash dispenser A machine that provides bank customers with 24-hour cashier service. To use the machine, you insert your plastic identification card and log in with a special password code. The machine's video display screen asks you questions; you use the keyboard to answer. Automatic cash dispensers let you draw out money, transfer cash from one account to another, and check your balances — all via the bank's computer.

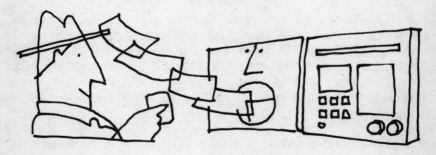

Automation The control of machines and processes by automatic devices. Examples of automation include automatic cash dispensers, robots on automobile assembly lines, and photo-electric 'eyes' that open doors for you. Automation can free us from many routine chores that may be dull, boring or even dangerous to people.

Babbage, Charles (1792–1871) Known as the father of computing, Babbage was the first person ever to conceive of and design a programmable computer. First, he designed the Difference Engine – a machine to calculate tables of logarithms. Sophisticated as it was, the Difference Engine was merely a complex calculator – a machine designed to perform one single task.

Babbage's breakthrough was the Analytical Engine. Here Babbage conceived of a steam-driven machine that could be directed or programmed to do any task the user wanted it to do. The obvious and cumbersome way of accomplishing this would have been to design a separate part of the machine to carry out each task. But Babbage's machine could switch from one task to the next just by ordering some changes in the workings of its internal components. In this sense it was truly a programmable computer – the world's first.

Babbage never got either machine to work. He did, however, invent two devices that were manufactured in his lifetime: the speedometer and the locomotive cowcatcher.

Backing store Also known as *bulk store*. A back-up to the computer's main memory. Backing store can hold more information, but it takes longer to get to the information in backing store. Examples of backing stores include floppy disks, hard disks and magnetic tapes.

Bandwidth A measure of how fast a telephone line or other communications link can carry information. It is measured in bits per second, or *baud rate*. The word comes from radio engineering.

Bar codes A way of putting numbers on groceries, books, and so forth so that computers can read them. (See *Universal Product Code*.)

BASIC Stands for Beginner's All-purpose Symbolic Instruction Code. BASIC is a simple, easy-to-learn, easy-to-use language that is very similar to ordinary written English. BASIC is supplied with most home computers and is probably the most popular language for home, educational and commercial applications.

Batch processing In batch processing, you write out your entire program in advance, usually on punched paper cards or paper tape. You then hand it to the computer operator, who runs programs in batches, and come back later to pick up your results — usually a computer print-out sheet. If there is an error, you must retype part of the program and hand it back to the operator for processing.

In batch processing, you don't have a question-and-answer type conversation with the computer as you would if you were using a terminal with keyboard and video display. Nowadays, batch processing is usually reserved for handling routine information processing such as payrolls, standardized test scores and domestic bills. Home computers have terminals that allow for a conversational or an interactive type of processing.

Baud rate A unit of measure of the speed of data transmission roughly equal to one bit per second. Some typical baud rates for data transmission equipment are 50, 110, 150, 300, 600, 1200, 1800, 2000, 2400, 4800, 7200, 9600 and 19,200. The higher the baud rate, the faster your system can transmit or receive information.

Bead A bead is a small part of a program written to perform a specific job. Beads can be developed individually and then strung in 'threads' to form a complete program. (See also *modular*.)

Benchmark A test to see how well a computer system does certain jobs under certain conditions.

(In land surveying, a bench mark is a mark made on a rock, tree or other stationary object used as a reference point by the surveyor.)

Binary number system Also known as *binary code*. This is the numbering system with which the computer counts. It has only two digits – 0 and 1.

We humans use a numbering system that has ten digits (the decimal system) because we can count on our ten fingers. The computer uses a two-digit numbering system because its electronic circuits can either be on or off – voltage or no voltage flowing through the circuit. On corresponds to the digit 1 and off corresponds to the digit 0. In a sense, the computer counts on its two 'electronic fingers' – on and off.

In our decimal system, each place or column represents ten times the value of the place to its right. In the number 245, 4 represents 40 (4 times 10) and 2 represents 200 (2 times 100) because of their respective positions.

In the binary system, each place or column is twice the value of the place to the right. The value of each position is shown below:

$$\overline{16} \quad \overline{8} \quad \overline{4} \quad \overline{2} \quad \overline{1}$$

Placing a 0 in a column indicates a zero value; placing a 1 in the column indicates a full value. To write 12 in binary code, you add 8 plus 4:

$$\frac{0}{16} \quad \frac{1}{8} \quad \frac{1}{4} \quad \frac{0}{2} \quad \frac{0}{1}$$

Here are the binary codes for the numbers 0 to 12:

decimal system	binary system
0	00000
1	00001
2	00010
3	00011
4	00100
5	00101
6	00110
7	00111
8	01000
9	01001
10	01010
11	01011
12	01100

Addition in binary code is easy. Just add the digits in columns, the same as you would ordinary numbers. The rules for binary addition are: $0+0 = 0$, $0+1 = 1$, $1+0 = 1$, and $1+1 = 10$. Let's write down 3 and 5 from the list of binary numbers, add them together and see what we get.

$$\begin{array}{r} 00011 \\ +\ 00101 \\ \hline 01000 \end{array} \qquad \begin{array}{r} 3 \\ +\ 5 \\ \hline 8 \end{array}$$

The answer is, of course, 01000 — the binary code for 8.

Bionics   Remember Steve Austin, television's 'Six Million Dollar Man'? When Steve lost an arm and both legs in a plane crash, they were replaced with artificial robotic limbs that looked and worked much like the originals.

In the field of bionics, scientists try to design and build machines that have the same characteristics and perform the same functions as living things. While not as advanced as the television version, real bionic

devices have replaced limbs and organs in many people. There are bionic arms, bionic legs, bionic hips . . . even bionic eyes and hearts. A related area is the science of cybernetics.

Bit Short for *binary digit*. A bit represents the smallest possible unit of information — a 1 or 0, a presence or absence of voltage, true or false, black or white — any two opposites. Computers handle information as bits by representing a bit as an on or off voltage in a circuit.

Bit diddling Computers handle information in groups of bits called words. Sometimes, words don't contain as many bits as they could; this wastes space when words are stored in the computer's memory. Bit diddling helps programmers make better use of storage by packing extra bits into the unused portions of computer words.

Some computer people think the technique is more trouble than it's worth, and so they named it bit diddling, as the verb 'to diddle' can mean to waste time.

Black box A black box is any machine whose inner workings are a mystery to the user. A pocket calculator is a good example of a black box: people who use one care only that it works and not *how* it works. (How many students in your class can clearly explain how pocket calculators do addition and multiplication?) Many business executives view computers as black boxes. They say, 'I don't have time to learn about computers. My only concern is that it helps me manage my

business.' When you think about it, the average person views almost all modern machines — cars, planes, microwave ovens, video games, telephones — as black boxes.

Block Just as your block or street is a set of separate homes treated as a single place ('he lives on my block'), a block in the computer is a group of smaller pieces of information (words or records) treated as a single unit of information to be moved from place to place. The blocks in a computer may all be the same length, or they may be different lengths. *Blocking* is putting together blocks from individual words or records.

Blow Also known as *blast* or *burn*. To put information into a special type of computer memory known as a programmable read-only memory (PROM).

Board A rectangular sheet on which the circuits of the computer are mounted. The board, in turn, is mounted on a chassis. A *circuit board* contains the circuitry of a microprocessor — the device that is the brains of most home computers. A number of circuit boards may be mounted on what is known as a *mother board*.

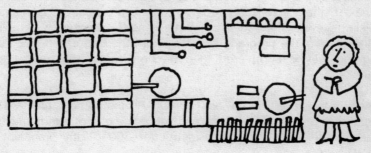

Boole, George (1815–1864) Boole was the first person to show that logic is a branch of mathematics, not philosophy. He used mathematical symbols to indicate logical operations ('compare these two statements', 'prove this conclusion', 'take this action') rather than quantities (sums and numbers). This thinking laid the foundation for today's modern computers, machines that translate real-life problems into mathematical terms.

Bootstrapping Without a program in its memory, a computer can do nothing, not even read in a program from cassette or floppy disk. Yet when you switch it on, the computer's memory is exactly that: empty. Thus the machine has to have some special circuitry to get it started when it is switched on, and this process is called 'bootstrapping' (sometimes 'booting'), from the joke about how difficult it is to pick oneself up by one's own bootstraps.

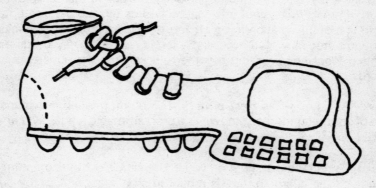

Bottom up technique In this programming technique, the writing of a computer program is broken up into several smaller parts, or modules. The most basic or *bottom level* module is written and tested first. Then the next highest level module is written. The procedure is repeated until all the levels of modules are written and the program is complete. In other words, the program is written from the bottom up. Each step along the way is completed to perfection before the next step is written.

Branch Also called 'jump' or 'GOTO'. An instruction that tells the computer to break out of the normal sequence of a program and carry on elsewhere, as in 'Branch to instruction 300'. Many branches are *conditional*, such as 'IF X = 5 THEN GOTO 200'. If the value of X is 5, this will cause a branch to instruction 200; if X is anything else, the program will carry on with the next instruction as normal.

Breadboard A crude, experimental model of a device, used to test whether the design will work as is or will need to be changed before the final version is built. Breadboard models help computer manufacturers detect and correct flaws in design before the computer hits the assembly line.

Breakpoint The point in a computer program where the sequence of instruction is interrupted. This interruption may be caused by an instruction written into the program or some action taken by the computer operator. During the interruption, the operator reads the print-out and checks the program for errors. After he's finished, the program starts up where it left off.

Bridgeware Computer components and programs used to translate instructions and information written for one type of computer into a format that another type of computer can understand. This is necessary because computers made by different manufacturers often speak different languages.

Brute-force approach When you can solve a problem with a precise set of mathematical equations and logical operations, mathematicians say you have found an elegant solution. Another way to solve problems is to guess at a rough answer, see how close to the solution you get with that answer, and keep guessing until you arrive at a solution that's

close enough for your purposes. Mathematicians call this the brute-force approach. Computers are especially good at the brute-force approach because they can do many repetitive calculations in a very short period of time.

Bubble memory A type of computer memory that stores information as microscopic magnetic bubbles on a thin wafer of garnet or other silicate material (silicates are semiconductors and the main ingredient of sand, glass and brick). Bubble memory can store a great deal of information in a very thin space. A magnetic field shifts the position of the bubble on the wafer to alter the contents of the memory.

Bubble sort A sorting technique used by a computer to put things in order.

Let's say you wanted to use this technique to sort four children's blocks. To stack them in order from the biggest to the smallest (with the biggest block on the bottom), compare the first two blocks from the bottom of the pile up. If the largest of the two is on the bottom, we leave them. But since it is not, we switch them.

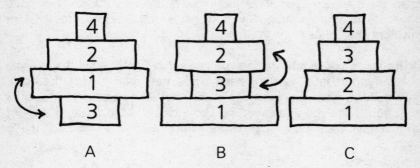

Now compare the second and the third blocks from the bottom. Since they are not in order, switch them. Move up the stack and compare the third and the fourth blocks. They are in order, so we leave them. The bubble sort gets its name from the fact that the sorting moves up the pile just as a bubble floats up through a glass of soda. We've floated up to the top of our pile of blocks, and you can see that the sort is finished and the blocks are stacked in the desired order. Usually you have to go back to the bottom and go through the pile several times before it is in order.

Because it can be time-consuming, the bubble sort is useful for sorting only a small number of items. For larger sorts, the computer uses other techniques, such as the partition sort.

Bucket brigade device   Also known as a *charge coupled device*. A type of storage technology that shifts stored information by transferring a charge of electric current from one capacitor in the device to the next — like passing a water bucket along a fire-fighting line from one fireman to another. The capacitors in this device are in high-density integrated circuits.

Buffer Sometimes one machine can send information faster than another machine can receive it. If this is the case, a buffer may be placed between the two machines. The buffer receives information from the speedy machine, holds it temporarily and then feeds it to the slower machine at a rate the machine can handle. The buffer may be either a segment of the computer's memory or part of another device.

Bug An error, defect or other problem that prevents the computer from working properly. Software bugs are errors in programs; hardware bugs are faults in equipment. *Debugging* – eliminating these errors and defects – can be a troublesome, time-consuming task; it can also be a fascinating game of detective work.

Burn-in Computers and electronic components are screened for flaws or early failures by running the circuits at elevated temperatures in some sort of oven. In a typical burn-in test, components might be run continuously for a week at 122°F. This testing regime causes weak links in the circuit to burn out; the manufacturer then replaces the failed circuitry with parts that will withstand the test.

Bus In any large city, buses move along different routes to take riders to many destinations.

In the computer, a bus is a group of wires. Information flows along one or more of the wires to reach a specific destination. Buses are

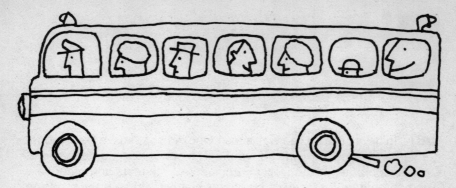

used to connect microprocessors with memory or with terminals, telephone lines and other outside devices.

Bush, Vannevar (1890–   ) In 1930, Bush built a computer that could solve complex calculus problems. His was the first computer to use electronic components instead of mechanical levers and gears to perform calculations and store information. (Bush's computer used radio valves to store information as a voltage.) Some say that Bush, not Charles Babbage, is the true father of modern computing because Bush was the first to build an electronic, general all-purpose computing machine.

Byte The amount of information used in a computer to store one character: a letter, figure, punctuation mark or other symbol. Most computers use bytes that are eight bits long, handling all information in byte-sized chunks.

C

CAD In days of old, a cad was a man who did not behave like a proper gentleman (as in 'Oh, you cad, you!'). The computer-age definition of CAD is Computer-Aided Design. Engineers, architects and others are using computers (particularly computer graphics) to help them design everything from aeroplanes and apartment houses to zips and zeppelins. With the computer, an engineer can study the effects of tornadoes and hurricanes on a bridge that hasn't been built yet. Or an interior decorator can walk inside a room that doesn't even exist by creating a picture of the room on a computer graphics terminal.

CAFS Stands for Content-Addressable File Store. A kind of computer storage device, usually using hard disks, that includes special hardware for searching for information in the store. This means you do not have to know where information is in order to find it, nor do you have to go to the trouble of constructing an index. You could write a computer program to do the searching but it would be very slow.

CAL or Computer-Aided Learning The use of computers in schools and training colleges to help people learn. The computer can display information for you, ask you questions, check your answers, and adjust the speed of the teaching to how well you are progressing. CAL can be used for teaching languages, maths, history, metal working, and a host of other subjects.

Calculator A hand-held or desk-top device used to do arithmetic and some simple logical functions. A calculator is essentially an electronic abacus or adding machine. Each operation must be punched in manually. A computer, on the other hand, can be programmed to follow a long sequence of written instructions with no outside help. Also, computers are more flexible than calculators since they can be programmed to perform just about any task. Calculators are limited by what their circuits allow them to do.

CAM or Computer-Aided Manufacture The use of computers in factories (often in conjunction with CAD). Products can be designed by computer, and instructions can then be fed directly to the machines that actually make the products. Other computers can be used to keep track of raw materials, orders, sales and costs. Plenty of people are still needed to supervise and tend the machines, however.

Canned programs Like canned beans, canned programs are prepared, ready-to-use products that you can buy right off the shelf. Canned programs are written for users who are not programmers and don't wish to create their own programs. Cartridges for home video games are a good example of this type of program. All canned programs are written to handle specific applications.

Cartridges Home video games come in the form of plug-in cartridges. The cartridges contain software permanently stored in miniature computer circuitry. They're convenient, easy to use, soundless, and you can't erase them. Other programs besides video games are available on cartridges. However, not all computers are designed to accommodate them.

Cassette tape   Have you ever seen a person wearing headphones in the street? Chances are the person was listening to music recorded on a cassette. The tape in the cassette is coated with a magnetic film, and the music is recorded in the form of varying voltages. Circuits in the cassette player convert these voltages back to musical tones.

Cassette tapes can also be used to store information for the computer. Computer data is stored on the tape as two different tones corresponding to the binary computer-code digits 0 and 1. Different tone patterns form words in this code.

Cassette tape is a relatively inexpensive computer memory medium. But tapes are slow-playing and easily damaged. What's worse, you have to search the tape in sequence to find a particular piece of information, just as you have to use 'rewind' or 'fast forward' to find a particular song on a cassette recording of a record album. That's why most computer manufacturers and users prefer to store information on a storage medium called a floppy disk.

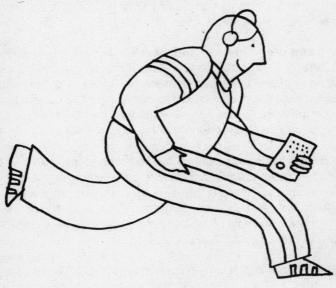

Casting out nines   A technique for making sure that the computer is correctly reading the numbers you feed into it. In casting out nines, you divide a number by nine and check the remainder; the remainder is the desired result of this operation. Performing casting out nines on 31, we divide 31 by 9: 9 goes into 31 three times with a remainder of 4. If the result was not 4, we would know that the computer was somehow not reading 31 as 31.

CCD or Charge-Coupled Device   See *bucket brigade device.*

Central Processing Unit (CPU)   The CPU is the electronic nerve centre or 'brain' of the computer. It is here that mathematical equations are solved and logical decisions are made. The CPU consists of three parts:

● Accumulators gather pieces of information taken out of memory and store them temporarily within the CPU itself. (See *accumulator.*)

● Control sections retrieve program instructions from memory, decode them and carry them out.

● The arithmetic/logic unit (ALU) performs the actual mathematical and logical functions. This is the unit that multiplies and divides, or decides which of two quantities is greater.

Chaining   Let's say a particular computer program is too big to fit into the computer's main memory all at once. We can get around this problem by dividing it up into several small programs and getting them to *chain*: that is, when the first is finished, it automatically calls in the next program and starts it running, and so on through the sequence.

Channel   A connection between the computer and a terminal or other external device. The computer and the terminal transmit information over the channel.

Character   A character is a single letter, figure, symbol or space and requires one byte of computer memory.

Character Addressable Storage Device   Also known as *Variable Word Length Storage.* Computer memory in which each character has one unique location in memory with its own address.

Check character A means of finding errors in the data fed into a computer. If you look at the back of this book, you will see a number called the ISBN, for International Standard Book Number. This appears on nearly all books nowadays, and is used for ordering copies. The last digit of the ISBN is not actually part of the number, but is a check character, worked out from the other digits by a mathematical formula. If the number is typed into a computer incorrectly, the computer sees that the number does not match the check character and will produce an error message. Check characters are used for many other purposes in computing today.

Checkpoint When a program reaches the checkpoint, all the details concerning the state and progress of the program are recorded into the computer memory. If a failure takes place and the program stops running, you can use this record to reconstruct the running of the program just as it happened, right up to the last checkpoint.

Cheshire Cat store Also known as *regenerative* or *dynamic memory*. Information stored in a Cheshire Cat memory will fade away in time unless it is refreshed. To refresh the memory, you must periodically read the data out and put it back again.

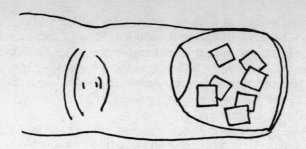

Chip Chips are tiny circuits that do the thinking in computers, calculators, microwave ovens and many other modern devices.

Chips are made of silicon (the main ingredient in beach sand) and typically have surface areas of a few tenths of a square inch; many chips could fit on your thumbnail. Thousands of microscopic electronic components are etched on the chip's surface, forming what is known as an integrated circuit.

Each component on the chip can represent a single binary digit as an on or off voltage. Because there are so many components on the chip, the chip can process thousands of pieces of information per second. For protection, chips are enclosed in ceramic or plastic packages. These packages include connectors that let the chips be plugged into circuit boards in various configurations.

CIM Stands for Computer Input from Microfilm. A form of *optical character recognition* that allows a computer to read information stored on microfilm and process it.

Circuit A collection of electronic components, transistors, resistors, capacitors, etc., that carry out a particular function. Computers contain many thousands of circuits.

Clock The clock on your kitchen wall keeps track of time in units that people can deal with — seconds, minutes and hours. Computers also need to know what time it is. But because they think and act faster than we do, their clocks keep track of smaller units of time; the clock in a home computer divides a second into a million different parts. Every millionth of a second, the clock sends out a pulse. Timed pulses keep all the various functions of the computer working together and on time.

Closed loop A loop is a sequence of instructions that the computer repeats until a certain condition is satisfied. When the condition is met, the computer moves on to the next step in the program. A closed loop is a continuous loop from which there is no escape; the computer performs the sequence of steps over and over until the operator intervenes. Here's an example of a closed loop.

Step 1: Electric light fails.
Step 2: Call electrician.
Step 3: Electrician rips out skirting board to repair cable.
Step 4: Call carpenter to repair skirting board.
Step 5: Carpenter puts nail through electric cable.
Step 6: Go to Step 2.

CMOS Short for Complementary Metal-Oxide Semiconductor. Pronounced 'see-moss'. CMOS is a semiconductor that uses very little power. The primary application of CMOS semiconductors is in cars, satellites, aeroplanes and portable devices. They are also used in battery-operated computer memory systems.

COBOL Stands for COmmon Business Oriented Language. COBOL is a computer language for business applications, sending bills, taking care of the payroll, keeping track of stock, etc. COBOL is a good language for handling information storage and retrieval; it is not very useful for complex scientific calculations.

Colossus Colossus was a computer built by the British during World War II to crack German coded messages. Computations were carried out by 2,000 valves and data was fed into the computer on punched paper tape. Colossus had a photo-electric reader that could scan the tape at a rate of 5,000 characters per second — fast even by today's standards.

COM Stands for Computer Output Microfilm. Computer output can be printed on microfilm. Microfilm output is faster and less expensive than paper. And with microfilm, you can print the contents of a newspaper on a single pocket-sized roll of plastic film.

Comment Comments are words written in a program that are not instructions to the computer but remarks to help a human looking at the program listing to understand what it is doing. For instance, in BASIC, everything on a line following the command REM (remark) is ignored by the computer: 100 REM CLOSING ROUTINE OF PROGRAM.

Communications processor A processor in a computer system that handles sending and receiving of information to and from terminals or other computers.

Compiler A program that translates the high-level programming languages you use into machine language that the computer can understand. Once the compiler translates your program statements into machine code, you can run that program as often as you like without having to translate it again. Using a compiler is like translating a book written in English into a foreign language before giving it to a foreigner to read. Another method for translating high-level language into machine language is the 'interpreter'. Compilers are more efficient than interpreters but harder to use.

Complement In mathematical terms, the opposite of something. The complement of off is on; the complement of 0 is 1; the complement of (binary) 1001011 is 0110100. Most computers have an operation to complement a byte or word, which would mean taking, say, 11000110 and producing 00111001.

Computer A computer is a machine that processes information according to a set of instructions stored within the machine. The computer manipulates the information and produces new information as a result — without any help from a person. By changing the instructions stored within the computer, you can make the computer do many different tasks. Computers help us write, keep track of things and perform complex calculations.

Every computer consists of the following parts:

● Input device — a keyboard, paper tape reader or other device that lets you put information into the machine.

● Processor — the part of the computer that manipulates the information.

● Memory — the place where information and instructions are stored.

● Output device — a printer, video display terminal or other device that shows you the new information the computer has produced.

Some features unique to computers include:

● Speed — computers can process millions of pieces of information per second.

● Flexibility — computers are programmable. They can perform almost any information processing job that can be written out as a series of numbered steps.

Modern computers consist mainly of electronic circuitry. They have no internal moving parts and are very compact.

Computer graphics Pictures created by a computer on a video display screen, printer or other device. Today computers are capable of producing very sophisticated graphics including movies, colour illustrations and three-dimensional drawings.

Core A small doughnut-shaped piece of magnetic material, about the size of a pin-head, used to store a single *bit* of information. If it is magnetized in one direction it represents a zero, and in the other direction, a one. Until a few years ago all computer main memories were made out of cores; now cores have been replaced by memories made out of semiconductors, many thousands of *flip-flops* or capacitors held in integrated circuits.

Core dump To dump or transfer the contents of a computer's brain memory to an output device or to another memory medium. The term originated in the days when *all* main memories were core memories.

That's not the case any more, but for old times' sake, a memory dump is still called a core dump.

Corruption Corruption occurs when information is accidentally lost, changed or disorganized by equipment failure or an error in a program.

CP/M One of the best-known operating systems for microcomputers. An advantage of using CP/M is that programs written on your computer with CP/M will run on a different computer if it also has CP/M.

Cps Short for characters per second – a measure of the speed of a printer or other device.

Crash A computer crashes when it breaks down because of an equipment fault or programming error.

A *head crash* occurs when the 'head' (the part of a floppy disk drive that picks up information) accidentally hits the disk surface. It's like dropping the tone arm on a record.

Crippled mode When part of a computer breaks down, the system can continue to operate at a reduced capacity. This is the crippled mode. (See also *graceful degradation*.)

CRT Stands for Cathode Ray Tube. The CRT uses a beam of electrons to produce images on a display screen. Images appear as dots, lines, blips and shaded areas. CRTs are used in oscilloscopes, word processors, radar displays, computer screens and television sets.

Cursor A blip or mark that appears on the computer screen to indicate position. When you're working with words or numbers on the screen, the cursor shows where you're making a correction or entering new information. (This kind of cursor may flash steadily to help you identify your location on the screen.)

In video games, the cursor is the character you can control with a joy stick. Pac-Man, for example, is a cursor.

Cybernetics The science which studies systems, such as animals and computers, that can control themselves. The simplest kind of mechanism of this sort is a speed governor on a steam engine. Animal nervous systems and weapons guidance are very much more complicated. The name comes from the Greek word *kubernetes*, which means steersman.

Cycle When a computer carries out an instruction in a program, it does so using a three-step cycle. The steps are:
1. Fetch – put the program instruction into the computer's processing unit.
2. Decode – translate the instruction into computer language.
3. Process – perform the actual operation.

D/A Stands for Digital-to-Analog. Conversion of signals from the digital or discrete format that computers use to the continuous analog signals that occur in the real world. A D/A converter lets computers drive speakers, motors and other machines.

Daisy chain Any child knows that daisies can be linked together to form a chain. And computer memory chips can be linked too. In a daisy chain, computer memory chips are connected so that signals move from one chip to the next in sequence. A series of programs can be accepted by each chip, one after another.

Daisy wheel An interchangeable typing element used in certain printers. Characters on the element are raised outlines at the ends of spokes sticking out of a central rod, like petals on a daisy. The rod rotates at high speed; when the desired character is in position, a hammer flies out and hits it. The outline strikes the paper through an inked ribbon, and the character is typed on the page. Daisy wheels give you 'letter quality' printing that looks as if it were produced on the best electric office typewriter. This printing is much sharper than the 'computer quality' printing produced by a dot matrix printer.

Data   Data is any kind of information put into, processed by, or taken out of a computer. Data processing is what the computer does when it sorts, manipulates and stores information.

Grammatically speaking, data is plural; datum is the singular form. But most computer users prefer to use data as both a singular and a plural noun.

Data bank   One or more data bases held on a computer so that many people can have access to them, and often open to the general public.

Data base   A large collection of information on one subject held in a computer and usually organized into a complicated structure, with the different items of information linked together.

Data base management system (DBMS)   Programs that enable users to build data bases, feed information into them, and get it out again.

Data entry operator   The person who has the job of entering data into a computer using a keyboard, punched cards, paper tapes, magnetic tapes or other storage media. Also called 'data preparation operator'.

Data processing   Another name for computing.

Deadly embrace   When two processes compete for the same device in the computer at the same time, the computer becomes deadlocked. The conflict must be resolved before the computer can resume its normal operation. There are three ways of getting out of a deadly embrace:
1. Remove one of the processes competing for the computer's resources.
2. Allocate the computer's resources on a priority basis.
3. Incorporate tie-breaking circuitry that can resolve conflicts as they arise.

Debugging   Finding the errors in a computer program – see *bug*.

Decade   A group of 10 storage locations – 10 places in memory, each of which can hold a single computer 'word'.

Decimal system The numbering system that people use to count. It has ten digits (0, 1, 2, 3, 4, 5, 6, 7, 8, 9), probably because we have ten fingers on which to count. The value of a digit depends on its place in a number; each place has ten times the value of the place to its right:

$$\frac{3}{1000} \quad \frac{6}{100} \quad \frac{2}{10} \quad \frac{1}{1}$$

As you can see, the value of 3,621 is (3×1000) plus (6×100) plus (2×10) plus (1×1): 3000+600+20+1=3,621.

Computers don't have fingers on which to count. They have electric circuits which can be only either on or off. As a result, they count using a numbering system based on two values: the binary number code.

Deck A pack of punched computer cards that can contain a program or a 'file' of information.

Dedicated A computer or other machine assigned to one particular user or application.

Delete To cross out or remove: as in 'deleting' a character typed in error.

Destructive read To read information is to retrieve it from memory. In a destructive read, the act of reading the data erases it from memory. This is what happens when you read data from a core memory.

Diagnostics A set of programs for testing a computer. Sometimes you run these; sometimes the computer can run them itself and tell you if something is wrong. Some computers can even correct problems themselves once they have been detected!

Dial-up A user dials up when he uses a telephone to make a connection between his remote terminal and a central computer. Dial-up eliminates the need to have the terminal connected to the computer at all times, since the user can plug in to the computer with a single phone call.

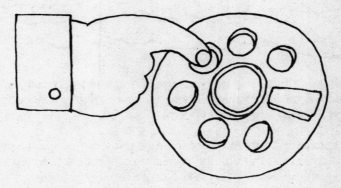

Digital Digital signals have discrete states, separate and distinct values; *analog* signals are continuously variable. A flight of steps is digital; a ramp, analog.

In most computers, digital logic has only two distinct states – 1 and 0, on and off voltage. But it can have up to 16 separate states in some devices.

Digital computer A computer that stores, transmits and manipulates information (numbers, symbols, letters and words) as binary code — digital information that has either a value of 1 or 0. The majority of computers in use today are digital; only a few are analog computers.

Diode A semiconductor component that allows electric current to flow in only one direction.

DIP Stands for Dual-In-line Package. An integrated circuit housed in a protective casing that includes two rows of pin connections for plugging the chip into a circuit board.

Direct access When you want to find a particular song on a cassette tape, you must run through the beginning of the tape to find or access the songs in the middle. This is known as sequential access.

With a record album, you can play the song immediately by lifting the tone arm and placing it where the song is recorded on the record's surface. This is direct access.

Many computer systems store information on floppy disks in much the same way that records store music. And like records, the information on disks can be accessed directly. You can go straight to the data you seek without having to search through the entire memory. Naturally, that's much faster than sequential access.

Direct address The true address of a memory location, held in a register, as opposed to an *indirect address*.

Display As a verb, what the computer does when it shows information to the user, either on the screen or by printing it out. As a noun, any sort of device for doing this, be it a video screen, a liquid crystal display, light-emitting diodes, or other kind.

Distributed processing The use of many small computers, connected together in a network or separate, instead of one big computer. With the falling cost of microcomputers, distributed processing with its flexibility and closeness to the end user has become very popular.

Dot matrix printer The dot matrix printer forms letters by printing them as patterns of dots within an area. The area is usually 7 by 9 dots, or 5 by 7 dots as shown below:

> The matrix printer prints the number '2' as a pattern of dots in a 5 by 7 grid.

There are two types of matrix printers:
- Impact printers — small needles form letters by striking the paper through an inked ribbon.
- Nonimpact printers — a spray jet of ink or a pulse of light or heat on sensitive paper forms the printing.

Matrix printing looks as if it was printed by a computer. Its quality is not as high as daisy-wheel letter-quality printers. However, matrix printers are cheaper.

Down A computer that is down is a computer that is not operating. It may be down because of a 'bug', 'crash', power failure or other problem. Or it may be down intentionally if the user does not need to do any computing for the time being.

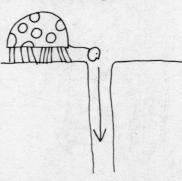

Down-time The period during which the machine is not operating because of a failure in the system.

Drift The output of an electric circuit tends to change slowly over a period of time. This is known as drift. Causes of drift include fluctuations in system voltage and changes in environmental conditions. Drift can cause analog computers to make errors, so the circuits in these computers are designed to correct for drift.

Drop-out A drop-out is a system failure that occurs during the time that a computer is putting information into or taking information out of a magnetic storage device. Bits of information are lost in the process. The opposite of drop-out is *drop-in* – the accidental generation of unwanted bits of information while the computer is transferring information to or from its magnetic memory. Drop-out is often caused by a scratch, blemish or particle lodged on the magnetic recording surface.

Dry run Before a program is run on the computer, the programmer may sit down with pencil and paper and go through the steps in the program by hand. He will do the calculations and record the results to make sure the logic of the program is correct. In a sense, the programmer proofreads his instructions in much the same way that an editor proofreads a manuscript, going through it page by page to find and correct mistakes.

Dummy routine In bridge, the dummy is the silent partner; in computers, it's the silent *routine* — a set of programming instructions that takes up space but does not actually do anything.

In some situations, the structure or setup of a progam may require a subset of instructions to be included, even though you don't need them. So, the programmer writes in a dummy routine to satisfy the structural requirement of the program.

As soon as the program enters the dummy routine, it is instructed to exit the routine and return immediately to the main program. Think of the dummy routine as the fourth chair in the dining room set of a family of three. It serves no real purpose, but the set wouldn't be complete without it.

Dump An operation in which the contents of a computer's memory are transferred to another memory or to an output device such as a line printer. Dumping clears the memory and stores its data elsewhere.

Dump and restart A technique for restarting a computer operation after it has unexpectedly stopped in the middle due to a programming error or equipment failure. You can start up at the point you left off; there is no need to go back to the beginning.

In a dump and restart, the computer records the progress of the program in its memory, then dumps (transfers) this record to an external memory medium such as a disk or a magnetic tape. To restart after a failure, you simply feed the record back into the computer's main memory to restore things to where they were when the computer stopped working. Normal operation can resume from that point on.

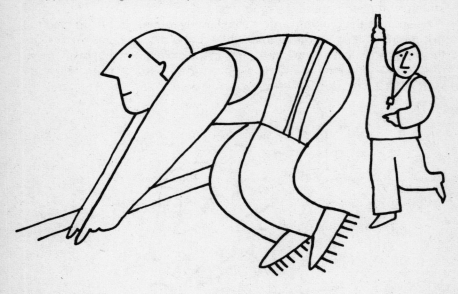

Duplex A data communications system that allows transmission of information in both directions at the same time. A telephone is a good example of a duplex device – you can hear a friend's stereo playing in the background as you speak to her.

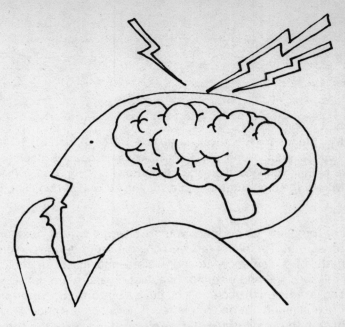

Dynamic memory A kind of semiconductor RAM that stores information as electric charges that leak away over time. Periodically the information must be read out and put back again. Also called *Cheshire Cat store.* Compare with *static memory.*

EAROM Stands for Electrically Alterable ROM. A kind of ROM that can in fact be erased and used again, using a special machine that employs higher voltages than the computer itself runs on. While the EAROM is in the computer, the information still cannot be changed or lost.

Editor A program that allows you to change written text on the computer screen. The editor lets you change the order of paragraphs, move parts of a sentence around, delete and insert material, and correct misspellings and errors in punctuation and grammar. Once all the editing is done on the screen, you push a button and a letter-perfect page of text is typed out on the printer. If revisions are necessary, you can go back to the computer, make the changes, and have the computer print out a perfectly typed revised manuscript. Used as word processors, computers with editors will soon make ordinary typewriters obsolete.

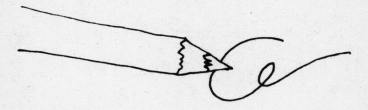

Effective address The effective address is the address of the location in memory that the computer wants to reach. In some addressing techniques, the computer must perform calculations on a 'base address' to come up with the effective address it needs.

Electronic Data Processing (EDP) The manipulation of information by computer. Also refers to the computer industry as a whole. When asked what he does for a living, a programmer might answer, 'I'm in EDP.'

Electronic funds transfer The exchange of money via a computerized telecommunications (telephone communications) system. Sending money by paper cheques is inefficient because it's slow, tedious and subject to errors. For transferring large sums of money, banks prefer a computerized system because it's quick and helps them keep track of where their money is. Every day, banks exchange hundreds of billions of pounds through electronic funds transfer.

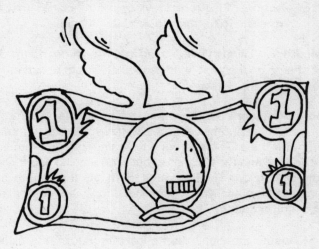

Electronic mail Various ways of sending letters electronically down wires, instead of having postmen carry pieces of paper around. For instance, you can compose a letter on a word processor which is connected to the telephone by a modem. If the person you are writing to also has such a word processor, you can send the letter down the phone line straight on to his word processor screen without ever having to make a paper copy of the letter at all. Electronic mail is faster than old-fashioned mail and is becoming cheaper, too.

Electronic Post A service offered to business firms by the British Post Office; in the U.S. it is called Electronic Computer-Originated Mail. Many companies have computers that print thousands of bills and the like every week and post them. The Post Office then has to transport the paper all around the country. With Electronic Post, these transport costs are saved because the firm gives the Post Office not the paper bills but a magnetic tape containing the data. The Post Office then sends the information by telephone line to centres near where the addresses of the bills live. It is only then that the bills are printed on to paper, and are then delivered by the local postmen.

Electronics Refers to the branch of science concerned with the behaviour of electrons. Electronic devices are machines that depend on valves or transistors to perform their main function.

Electrosensitive A kind of paper used in low-cost *dot matrix printers*. An electric charge on the print head causes the paper to darken, leaving a readable mark.

Emulation Sometimes people want to run programs on one computer that were written for another computer and would not normally work on a different machine. To get around this, a special program called an *emulator* is loaded into the computer that is now being used. This takes the program instructions and translates them into the correct language for that machine. In other words, it makes it look like, or *emulates*, the other kind of computer.

ENIAC Stands for Electronic Numerical Integrator And Calculator. A high-speed electronic computer built in 1946 at the University of Pennsylvania to calculate the way bombs and shells travel when they're fired. ENIAC contained 18,000 valves, 70,000 resistors, 10,000 capacitors, and weighed 30 tons. It could process information at a rate of tens of thousands of bits per second.

EPROM Stands for Erasable PROM. A kind of PROM that can be erased and used again. It usually has a glass window on the top of the chip, and can be erased by ultra-violet light from a special machine.

Erase When you erase a blackboard, you wipe it clean, removing all the information on it and leaving it blank. The same goes for computer

memory. When you erase the memory, you clear it of information and leave it blank.

Remember that all information is stored as patterns of the binary digits 1 and 0. Erasing memory returns all circuits to the no-voltage or 0 state.

Error message A statement from the computer telling you that you have made a mistake in programming or operating the machine. The computer does not know what it was you wanted to do; all it knows is that what you asked it was not possible, or was not intelligible.

Ethernet A kind of *local area network* developed by Xerox. It uses special coaxial cable strung out in one long line, as opposed to a *ring*.

Execute A computer executes a program when it performs all the operations specified by its instructions. A computer operator executes an instruction by causing the computer to run the program. To accomplish this, he might flip a switch, type a code on the keyboard, feed in a paper tape or take some similar action.

Expert system   A computer program, developed in the field of *artificial intelligence*, which does the job of a highly skilled human expert, such as a doctor, an engineer, an oil geologist, or a research chemist. Knowledge from these specialist people is fed into the computer in the form of hundreds or even thousands of rules about their subject, so that sometimes the computer can become even more expert than the human.

Exponent   In mathematics, a small number written at the upper right corner of another number to indicate that it is to be multiplied by itself. For instance 5^3 means $5 \times 5 \times 5$ or 125; 3 is the exponent. 10^6 is $10 \times 10 \times 10 \times 10 \times 10 \times 10$ or one million: 1,000,000. (See *floating point arithmetic*.)

Facsimile (fax) The process of scanning a picture or page of text and converting it to signals that can be sent over a telephone line or other communications channel. A machine at the receiving end picks up the signals and converts them back to their original form to produce a copy of the original image.

Fail soft A fail-soft computer system is designed to shut itself down in case of a serious error or fault. Fail-soft systems remain shut down until the defect is corrected, and they accomplish this with no loss of data and no additional damage to the system.

Fatal error An unexpected failure, 'bug' or other problem that occurs while the program is running. A fatal error prevents the computer from continuing to run the program. If the error is *nonfatal*, the program will proceed, but not correctly.

Feedback Feedback helps the computer to change its course of action based on the progress of its current operations. Feedback is the use of information produced at one step in a program to determine how the next step will proceed. In this way the computer can, in some ways, control its own actions.

Fibre optics The use of thin glass fibres, looking rather like fishing line, to transmit information, instead of copper wires. The data is sent down the fibre as a series of pulses of light; these can be sent at a very much higher rate than can electrical signals, and there is no problem of interference – the crackling noise you can get on the telephone or the radio.

Field A field is an area, an open space. As far as computers are concerned, a field is an area set aside in either a record (a collection of information stored in memory) or an instruction. It is used to contain a specific piece of information.

A school's computer system might have a complete record on each student. Different fields within the record would each contain specific pieces of information such as name, age, telephone number, year and class schedule.

FIFO (First-In, First-Out) A method of handling information that you store in the computer. With a First-In, First-Out system, the first piece of information you put into the computer will be the first piece of information you can take out.

To understand FIFO, pretend the computer is a hollow cardboard tube open at both ends, and that information is stored as ping-pong balls you insert into the tube at one end. As you keep stuffing balls into the tube, the first ball you put in will be pushed along the length of the tube until it pops out at the far end. This is how FIFO works.

FIFO can be used to serve as a buffer between two devices operating at different speeds. Each device is connected to a different end of the FIFO 'tube'. Information stored in this way is called a *queue* and is the opposite of a *stack* – as in *LIFO*.

Fifth Generation A speculative idea, originating from Japan, about the computers of the 1990s (the Fourth Generation supposedly being the computers of the late 1980s). These computers will, it is hoped, be able to understand human speech, talk in plain English, translate languages, such as English into Japanese and vice versa, and solve difficult human problems using large stores of knowledge. The Japanese government is spending large sums of money on research into these areas.

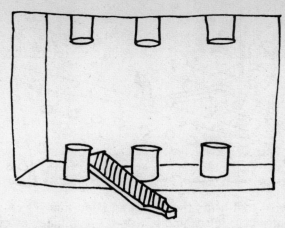

File If your parents work in an office, you may have seen how information is stored there in metal file cabinets. All papers covering one subject are put into the same cardboard file folder, which is then labelled and stored in the cabinet alphabetically.

Computers also store information under files, and these too have identifying labels or codes. A file is divided up into records, and each record is divided into fields.

File protect ring Often, computer files are stored on magnetic tape reels. The file protect ring is a detachable plastic ring that fits on the hub of the reel. When this ring is removed, it is impossible to record on the tape, and this prevents it from being accidentally erased.

Firmware Computer programs permanently stored in ROM or PROMs. Home video game cartridges are one example of firmware.

Fixed point arithmetic A way of doing arithmetic in which the decimal point is 'fixed'; that is, it always appears at the same point in the numbers the computer is working with.

Flag Many people use flags to keep track of things. Football linesmen raise their flags to mark the spot where the ball has gone out of play. And mountain climbers plant flags at the tops of mountains to show that they've been there.

Computers also use flags to keep track of things. In the computer, a flag is a single 'bit' of memory in the computer's brain (central

processing unit) that helps the computer keep track of certain conditions. The carry flag, for example, tells the computer whether it has carried the 1 when it is adding two numbers together. Most computers have several different flags to keep tabs on a variety of operations.

Flip-flop An electronic circuit which can be either on or off — no intermediate state is possible. Therefore, a flip-flop circuit can contain one piece or bit of information in binary form — on (1) or off (0). A pulse of electric current will change or flip this circuit to its other state.

Floating point arithmetic Many pocket calculators and computers can handle numbers of a limited size only. To get around this, computers represent numbers in scientific notation. In this notation, the number 900 would be written as 0·9 multiplied by 1000.

Now, 1000 can be written as 10×10×10. For convenience, we write this as E3. (In the same way, the number 100 (10×10) would be written as E2.) Therefore, in scientific notation, 900 is written as ·9 E3, which is 0·9×10×10×10.

You can see that scientific notation breaks the number into two parts: the fraction (·9) and the exponent (E3). (In fact, the E symbol stands for the word exponent.) Because the decimal point in the number changes or floats when the value of the exponent changes, this system is called floating point arithmetic.

Floppy disk (or disc) Also known as a diskette. A type of computer storage made from a plastic disk coated with magnetic material. Binary information is recorded on the disk's surface as patterns of magnetic charges.

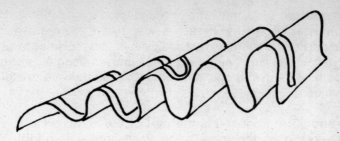

The disks are called floppy because they bend if you hold them by the edge. They come in standard sizes of 5¼- and 8-inch diameters (smaller disks, called mini-floppies, are also available). To use floppy disks, you need a piece of equipment known as a floppy disk drive.

Floppy disk drive A machine that plugs into your computer and lets you store information on floppy disks. Inside the drive, the disk spins at high speed while a record/play head (similar to the record/play head you see in tape recorders) takes information off the disk's surface and feeds it to the computer. The disk drive can also receive information from the computer and store it on the disk.

Flow chart A diagram that represents the sequence of events that takes place in solving a problem. Before a programmer writes his program in computer language, he draws a flow chart to make sure his logic is correct. Flow charts use simple line drawings to represent computer functions. A box, for example, symbolizes a computation, such as division or multiplication, while a diamond represents a test or a decision that has to be made.

Format The way information is laid out. You may be concerned with the format of the information printed out by your computer. Also, disks often have to have a format laid on them before they can accept your data, and the process of doing this to brand new disks is called 'formatting'.

FORTRAN Stands for FORmula TRANslation. A high-level computer language developed for scientific applications. FORTRAN is designed to do complex calculations and solve difficult problems in physics, maths, engineering and many other scientific fields. FORTRAN is so old now that it is widely regarded as obsolete.

Fragmentation Fragmentation occurs when information is placed in the computer's memory in such a way that there are a number of unused portions of memory that, individually, are too small to be useful. To solve this problem, you collect these unused fragments of memory and combine them into one large area that can be used to store more information.

Front-end The front-end is the part of the computer that the user works — keyboard, terminals, small processors and so forth. A front-end processor usually does simple, routine work such as sorting information or translating programs into machine language, while the main processor handles more difficult tasks — storage, program execution and mathematical calculations.

Function In languages such as BASIC, an operation in the computer that is not a command on its own but which must form part of another instruction. For instance, the Square Root function is SQR, but you cannot simply say SQR(25); you have to say PRINT SQR(25) or LET N = SQR(25).

G

Gallium arsenide A semiconductor material that is used in place of silicon in chips for advanced, high-speed circuits.

Gang punch In a gang punch, a card-punching machine makes many duplicates of a single original card. The machine reads the information from the first card and punches it on to a second card. Then it reads this information from the second card and punches it on to a third card. The process is repeated until the identical information is punched on to all the cards in a batch.

Garbage collection Pieces of information that you no longer need just waste space sitting in memory. Garbage collection is a technique that uses a program to search through the memory and throw out all unused, obsolete bits of information. It frees valuable memory space to receive and store more current information.

Gate An electronic circuit that performs a logical operation such as AND, OR, NOT, YES/NO, TRUE/FALSE and so forth.

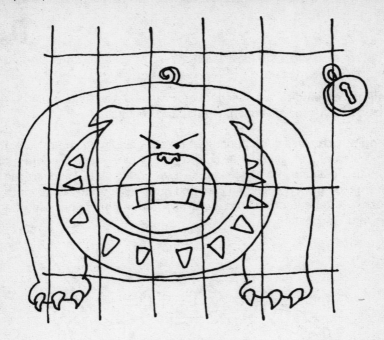

Gateway A switching centre that connects two independent computer systems or networks. For instance, Prestel has a gateway to various other computers belonging to travel firms or building societies. This allows you to use Prestel as a way of gaining access to those other computers.

Generation Like people, computers also have a generation gap. Today's computers are thousands of times smaller and millions of times faster than their predecessors of the 1930s and 1940s.
   Computer experts agree that there are three distinct generations of computers:
- First-generation computers are machines built with radio valves.
- Second-generation computers are machines built with transistors.
- Third-generation computers are machines built with integrated circuits.

GIGO Stands for Garbage-In, Garbage-Out. A warning that you cannot expect to get correct answers out of a computer if the information you feed in is wrong.

Glitch A glitch is an unexpected, unwanted electronic pulse in the computer that causes a program to make a mistake or fail altogether. Improper circuit design, airwaves, heat, thunderstorms, nearby electrical equipment or a momentary power surge can result in a glitch.

Graceful degradation Manufacturers construct computers so that the failure of a single part does not cause a complete system breakdown, but instead allows operation to continue at a reduced capacity. This is graceful degradation.

Grandfather tape Whenever you want to change the information on a magnetic tape, you produce a new, updated tape. However, it is a good idea to keep the old tape in case there is something wrong with the new one. Then when you make a still newer tape, it's still advisable to keep the two previous tapes. These tapes are called the Grandfather, the Father, and the Son.

Gulp A group of binary digits consisting of several bytes (a byte contains eight binary digits).

Hacker An American name for a computer fanatic; someone who lives, eats and breathes computers.

Half-duplex A data communications system that allows transmission in both directions but not at the same time. One example of a half-duplex communications system is the telegraph line: it can send or receive messages, but not simultaneously.

Handshaking People use a handshake to greet one another. And computers do too, only their version of handshaking is an exchange of information rather than a press of the flesh.

Before the user at computer terminal 'A' can transmit information to terminal 'B', he sends a handshaking message that asks, 'Are you ready to receive my information?' Terminal 'B' will respond either 'yes' or 'no', depending on whether he is ready to communicate. Once the

connection is made, handshaking is used to determine whether individual messages are received and understood by the recipient terminal.

Hard copy Computer output printed on paper. Hard copy provides a permanent record that the user can read and carry away with him.

Hard disk A computer storage medium that works in the same way as a floppy disk but which uses larger, rigid metal disks. Hard disks hold more information than floppy disks and are much more expensive. Some can be taken in and out of the computer and others are fixed inside permanently.

Hardware The physical components of the computer – the things made out of metal, plastic and wire. Hardware includes the keyboard, video display screen, memory storage devices, circuit boards and printer. (See also *software*.)

Head An electromagnet used to record, receive or erase information stored on magnetic tapes, disks, cassettes or drums. The *head gap* is the distance between the head and the magnetic surface.

Heuristic A mathematical word for a rule-of-thumb. One might be, 'If it looks like rain, take an umbrella.' Of course, you don't *have* to take an umbrella, but it is a good idea. Heuristic programming uses rules-of-thumb to tackle very difficult problems for which there is no complete solution or *algorithm*. Such problems include diagnosis of diseases, forecasting the weather, and playing complicated games like chess. (See also *artificial intelligence*.)

71

Hexadecimal A system of counting in sixteens, instead of tens as we do normally. It is used as a shorthand way of writing binary. It requires six more numerals than does decimal counting; these are A,B,C,D,E,F. Here are the numbers 1 to 20 in decimal, hexadecimal and binary:

decimal	hexadecimal	binary
0	0	0
1	1	1
2	2	10
3	3	11
4	4	100
5	5	101
6	6	110
7	7	111
8	8	1000
9	9	1001
10	A	1010
11	B	1011
12	C	1100
13	D	1101
14	E	1110
15	F	1111
16	10	10000
17	11	10001
18	12	10010
19	13	10011
20	14	10100

High-level languages These are sophisticated computer languages that closely resemble plain English. FORTRAN, COBOL and BASIC are three popular high-level languages. Although the computer must translate these high-level languages into machine language, they are easier to use than the more primitive assembly languages.

HIPO Stands for Hierarchy plus Input-Processing-Output. Like flow charts, HIPO is a tool that helps computer people write programs. Unlike flow charts, however, HIPO is more concerned with what is done than how it is done. HIPO diagrams consist of a series of blocks

containing text that describes the logic and goals of each step of the program.

Hollerith, Herman (1860–1929) In the late 1800s, Hollerith invented a machine to record the results of the U.S. Census. Hollerith's machine ran on electricity, and it was the first device to receive data on punched paper cards. Each card could hold 240 pieces of information. The code used to write information on punched cards is called the Hollerith code.

Home computer A hand-held or desk-top computer purchased for personal use. Today you can buy a good home computer for less than £100. Children and teenagers play video games and do homework with these computers. Adults use them to keep inventory of household items, figure out the income tax, balance budgets and pay the bills. All home computers contain a microprocessor.

Housekeeping Your family has to do a lot of routine housekeeping chores just to keep the house in order. So does the computer. Housekeeping is time spent by the computer to rewind tapes, clear memory, regenerate storage and handle other routine chores that keep it working smoothly.

Impact printer See *printer*.

Indirect addressing If you recall, the address is the location of a piece of information in memory. Usually, an address leads you directly to the place where you can find the information you need.

In indirect addressing, however, the address leads you to a memory location that contains yet another address. This second address gives you the location of the information you seek.

Indirect addressing is like mailing a letter to a post office box. The address of the box is not the real location of the person to whom you are writing. When the letter arrives in the box, it is then delivered to its final destination — the addressee's home.

Information life span Information doesn't stay current and useful for ever and its value changes as it gets older. A piece of information can be said to go through three distinct phases in its life:

● Dynamic information is fresh, current information. It is stored in the computer's main memory because users need to get to it quickly. Airline reservation information is dynamic information.

● Semidynamic information is still looked up from time to time, but it's no longer new. Last year's school reports are an example of semidynamic information. This data is usually stored on magnetic tape, disks or some other secondary storage medium.

● Static or archival information is old, out-of-date information. Usually stored on paper or microfilm, archival information can sit on a shelf or in a drawer without being looked at for years at a time.

Information technology A general term for the whole science of computing, transmitting data from place to place, and techniques for handling information.

Ink jet printer A kind of non-impact *printer* which makes marks on paper by spraying ink on to the paper in a tiny jet, controlled by electric charges.

Input The information that is going into a computer. Compare this with *output*.

Instruction A single order that tells the computer to carry out some specific task. An instruction in a program might tell the computer to operate a line printer, add two numbers together, store information in memory or perform any one of a number of other functions. Each instruction must be retrieved from memory, decoded and executed by the computer's central processing unit. A *program* is simply a series of instructions designed to solve a problem or accomplish a task.

Integer A whole number (2, 57) as opposed to a fraction or mixed numbers ($\frac{1}{4}$, $17\frac{1}{3}$). In a computer, all numbers are either integers or *real numbers*.

Integrated circuit (IC) A miniature electronic circuit imprinted or etched on the surface of a silicon chip. Components on the chip are linked by an imprinted pathway of conductive material rather than wires and soldered electrical connections.

Interactive In interactive computing, the user sits down at a terminal and has a 'conversation' with the computer. The computer asks questions, which are printed out on the video screen, and the user types in answers and instructions on the keyboard.

Interface A device that links two parts of a computer. Or, a device that links a computer with an accessory or with another computer.
  A man-machine interface is the link between the user and the computer. In interactive computing, this device is the terminal together with its associated software. A four-way joy stick is the control that serves as a man-machine interface between you and a Pac-Man arcade game.

Interpreter A program that translates the user's programming language (such as BASIC, FORTRAN or COBOL) into machine language code that the computer can understand.

The computer translates the programmer's language into machine language one statement at a time, in much the same way that a translator at the United Nations would translate Russian into English sentence by sentence. The interpreter's translations are not preserved, so a program must be reinterpreted every time it is used. This makes interpreters far less efficient than compilers. The advantage of interpreters is that they are easy to use.

Interrupt Sometimes users need to interrupt the computer while it is working on a problem and ask it to handle another task. To accomplish this, you send an interrupt signal to the computer's microprocessor. This signal causes the computer to put a hold on what it is doing and switch to a part of the program that can handle the special request. After the interruption has been taken care of, the computer resumes operation where it had left off when the interrupt signal was sent. If you expect many interruptions, you need to establish a set of interrupt priorities that tells the computer which interruptions it should handle first.

Inverter Also known as *NOT gate*. A logic circuit whose output is the reverse of the input: a 1 gives a 0, and a 0 gives a 1. Such a circuit performs the function of negation; that is, whatever comes out is the opposite of whatever goes in. If you say 'true' the inverter says 'false'; if you say 'yes' the inverter says 'no'.

ISAM Stands for Indexed Sequential Access Method. Certain information is best processed in sequence. Sales at a supermarket checkout counter, for example, are recorded in the order in which they are rung up. When data is processed sequentially, it is only natural to store it in the computer's memory sequentially. ISAM is a method of doing this.

In ISAM, each piece of stored information is labelled with an index code. The index tells the computer the approximate location of the information on the disk. The computer then searches that general area of the disk until it comes up with the data.

Jacquard, Joseph (1752–1834) In 1801, Jacquard invented a loom that used patterns of holes punched in cards to control the action of the loom as it wove thread into cloth. Eighty-five years later, Herman Hollerith used this punched-card technique to control a machine that stored and tabulated U.S. Census Bureau information. Jacquard's punched cards are still in use today for feeding data to computers.

Joy stick A lever that moves in all directions, the joy stick lets you move a cursor, or electronic blip, on the computer screen. In video games, cursors are used to avoid rolling barrels and ghosts, shoot down alien invaders or gobble up energy pills.

Jump Another word for *branch*.

K Stands for 1,000 (in the metric system, K stands for kilo, the prefix for 1,000 – a kilometre is 1,000 metres). You might say that the speed of a data communication line was 24 K baud, or 24 kilobaud. On the other hand, when you quote the size of a computer's memory in K bytes, each byte is not 1,000 but 1,024 (which is a power of two, coming from binary numbers). Thus a computer with 16 K of memory has 16,384 (16×1,024) bytes of RAM.

Sometimes, though, people mean bits, not bytes, and this can be confusing. A '64 K RAM' is a memory chip with a capacity of 65,536 bits.

Key A digit or digits used as a label that lets the computer locate or identify a collection of information (a record) stored in memory. The key is not necessarily attached to the record.

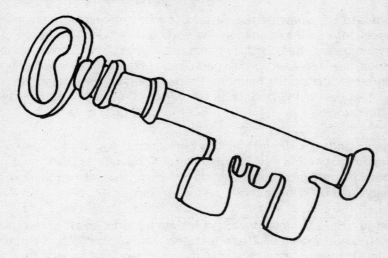

Keyboard A typewriterlike device used for entering information and instructions into the computer. The keyboard includes keys representing numbers, letters and symbols, plus special-function keys that instruct the computer to do specialized tasks such as interrupting a program or erasing the memory. The keyboard also has cursor control keys that control the position of the cursor (a movable electronic blip) on the screen.

Kips Stands for kilo instructions per second. A unit of measure of computing speed, a kips is equal to 1,000 operations performed per second. A small processor might do 500 kips, while a larger unit can be capable of 3,000 kips or more.

Kludge Have you ever watched anyone try to fix an old screen door with patches and tape? That's a kludge — a makeshift job of patching something together to correct a defect. Computer people also use kludges to fix errors. But a better way of fixing a program is to start again with a clean design; too many kludges make for sloppy computing. In the same way, when the screen door has too many holes in it, it is best to throw it away and replace it with a new one.

Label A word or number used to identify lines in a program — used especially in branch instructions. Can also be an identifier recorded at the beginning of a magnetic tape.

Language Language lets you communicate in written and spoken words. Computer languages are organized systems of words, phrases and symbols that let you communicate with the computer and tell it what to do. Popular computer languages include ALGOL, APL, BASIC, COBOL, FORTRAN and Pascal.

Laser printer A kind of non-impact printer that uses a computer-controlled laser beam to draw the characters (and pictures if you wish) on to an electrostatic drum, which then carries powdered ink on to the paper. Laser printers are fast, capable of very high-quality printing, and expensive.

LCD Stands for Liquid-Crystal Display. The display device commonly used in digital watches as well as in some small computers. Exotic materials called liquid crystals change the way they reflect light under the influence of tiny electric currents, and this effect can be used to form figures and letters.

Leapfrog test Remember the game of leapfrog, where you would jump from one kid's back to the next? Computers use a variation of this

game called 'the leapfrog test' to check out the information stored in different locations in memory. In such a test, the computer jumps or leapfrogs from one memory location to another until all locations have been tested.

LED Stands for Light-Emitting Diode. An electric device that emits light when current flows through it. LEDs on most pocket calculators are red, but orange, yellow and green displays are also available.

Leg The logical sequence of events in a routine or subroutine that is part of a larger program. Legs are the different paths the computer program can travel along, depending on which routines and subroutines it selects and follows.

Leibniz, Gottfried Wilhelm (1646–1716) In 1679, Leibniz perfected the binary code, the two-digit numbering system used by computers to count and keep track of things. Leibniz also constructed a mechanical calculating machine whose central component was a multiplier wheel with teeth of varying lengths. This same wheel was used in the electro-mechanical calculators of the 1960s.

In addition, Leibniz is well-known for inventing calculus.

Letter quality Describes computer printers that produce print-outs that look as if they were typed on a high-quality office typewriter. Letter-quality printers form letters by striking paper with a metal or plastic typing element through an inked ribbon. Many home computers are equipped with *dot matrix printers* that are less expensive than letter-quality printers but don't give the same quality typing.

Library program A good school library has all the books students need to study and do homework. In the same way, a computer has a library of the programs it needs to carry out your orders.

LIFO Stands for Last-In, First-Out. A device or way of handling information in which the most recent item put into memory is the first item you have to take out. (See *stack*.)

Light pen A device that lets you tell the computer what to do by touching the video screen.

At one end of the pen, a cable connects the pen with the computer. At the other end is a sensor that detects areas of light on the display. The sensor 'sees' an area, and the computer can determine where on the screen the tip of the pen is pointed. So, instead of typing information on a keyboard, you simply point the pen towards the word, phrase or drawing on the screen upon which you want the computer to act.

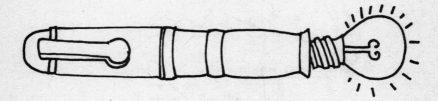

Line printer A large, fast impact printer that prints a whole line at a time, unlike a daisy-wheel printer which prints one character after another. Used mainly on mainframe computers.

Listing A complete program as printed out or displayed on the computer screen.

Liveware People needed to run the computer: operators, programmers, systems analysts, technicians, key punchers and other computer personnel.

Local area network or LAN A means of connecting computers, terminals and other devices that are within one building with high-speed links. Local area networks include *rings* and *Ethernets*.

Location A place in the computer's memory where a single item of information can be stored. The position of a location in memory is identified by its address.

Logical operation Mr Spock from the old 'Star Trek' television series was without emotion, and he based all his decisions on logical thought.

Logic is reason based on fact. If I am 1.7m tall, and the National Basketball Association says that all players must be at least 1.8m tall (it doesn't really), then logic says that I cannot play basketball for the National Basketball Association.

A logical operation expresses such reasoning in terms of mathematical equations and symbols. Logical operations manipulate and compare these symbols using logical operators such as AND, OR, NOT and NAND.

Logo A computer language for primary school children. Logo lets children use English-language statements to control the movement of a 'turtle' (represented as a triangle of light on the computer screen). For example, the command RIGHT 90 turns the turtle 90° to the right, while FORWARD 10 sends it ahead 10 millimetres. By moving the turtle, children can draw pictures, graphs and charts.

Log on/log off The routines you go through, such as giving passwords, when you start to use a time-shared computer and when you finish.

Loop A series of instructions the computer performs over and over again until a test shows that a specific condition is satisfied — at which point the computer ends the loop and goes on to the next step in the program.

In the *Sorcerer's Apprentice*, the apprentice to the wizard commanded magical servants to fill a tub with water, bucket by bucket. Unfortunately, he didn't tell them to stop when the tub was full, and they kept dumping buckets of water until the entire castle was flooded. You *must* tell the computer when to end the loop – otherwise you'll be trapped in a closed loop which goes on without end.

LSI Stands for Large Scale Integration. A technology in which tens of thousands of semiconductor devices are contained on a silicon chip about the size of the letter 'o' in this text.

M Stands for mega-, one million. In referring to computer memory, however, an Mbyte or megabyte is usually taken to mean 2^{20} or 1,048,576 bytes.

MAC Stands for Multi-Access Computing. A technique that allows a number of people to hold a conversation with a computer at the same time. MAC systems have anywhere from two to several hundred outlets that link the main computer to remote devices such as terminals, word processors, cash registers and consoles. (See also *time sharing*.)

Machine language A language consisting of words in binary number code that computers can understand. A statement in machine language might look like this: 1001101011010. As you can see, it would be difficult for people to write programs in this code. That's why computer people invented assembly languages and high-level languages that express information and instructions in phrases and words that people can understand. Special programs in the computer called assemblers, interpreters and compilers translate these languages into machine language so that the computer can understand them.

Macro In assembly language, certain sequences of instructions may be used several times in the same program or set of programs. Rather than write out the entire sequence every time you want to use it, you can replace the sequence with a *macro* – a single symbol or phrase that represents the sequence. When the assembler reads the macro instruction, it will automatically substitute the entire sequence of instructions the macro symbolizes.

Magneto-strictive effect You don't necessarily have to touch a piece of material to bend it or change its shape. Heat, for example, can cause a metal rod to expand. Magnetic fields can cause stress in materials, too. Materials physically affected by magnetic fields are called magneto-strictive. The stress in the material increases as the square of the applied magnetic field. This magneto-strictive effect is used to convert electrical signals to sound waves.

Mainframe A medium-sized or large commercial computer. Main-frames are fast, expensive, powerful and big; a single mainframe can take up an entire room and several full-time computer operators may be needed just to keep it running. Mainframes have more memory than home computers.

Main memory The internal memory of the computer. Main memory can be reached much faster than secondary storage devices that store information outside of the computer (these secondary storage devices include disks, tapes and cassettes).

Management Information System (MIS) In business, an MIS is a computer system that records and analyses everything that goes on in a big corporation. Its files include information on people, procedures, decisions, financial resources and facilities. The purpose of an MIS is to provide managers and executives with information to help them make better decisions, learn from their successes, avoid repeating mistakes and plan for the future.

Mark I The Harvard Mark I was the first fully automatic computer – the first machine to fulfil the requirements of Charles Babbage's Analytical Engine. Built in 1943 at Harvard, the Mark I was nearly 17m long and 2.5m high, and it contained 760,000 individual parts and 500 miles of wire. Its electro-mechanical relays, controlled by instructions

89

fed in on paper tape, could perform dozens of calculations per second. Construction of the machine was funded, in part, by IBM. The machine's designers called it the Automatic Sequence Controlled Calculator; the press dubbed it 'the electronic brain'.

Mask Information in the computer exists as patterns of the digits 0 and 1 — binary digits or 'bits'. A mask is a special pattern of bits that alters the positions of bits in other bit patterns. The mask can be used to select, ignore, set, or clear bit patterns.

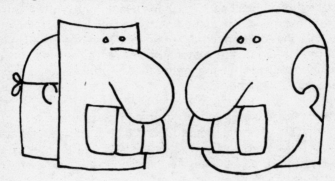

To understand how a mask can be used to select part of a pattern of a computer word, take a piece of paper the size of this page and cut an opening in the middle of it as long and as high as a single line of the text. Think of this page as computer information and of the paper as a mask. By placing the paper mask over this page, you can screen out most of the information and select only the portion of the text you want to read. This is how a mask works.

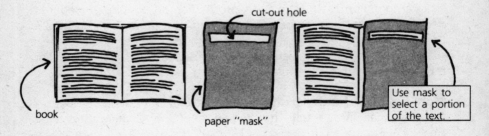

By placing the paper mask over the page (right), you can select a part of the text and block out the rest. This is how masking works in the computer.

Master card Computer users who write programs on punched cards carry all the cards for a single program or file of information together in a pack or deck of cards. The master card is a card in the pack that contains information on all of the other cards — the equivalent of a table of contents or index of a book. The master card is usually the first or last card in the deck.

Master/slave system In this type of system, a large central computer controls a number of smaller machines. Under the direction of the master, these slave computers may be assigned to carry out a variety of special tasks including the transmission, editing and processing of information.

Mathematical model Mathematical models use equations, numbers and symbols to represent real-life situations. A maths textbook asks you to translate word problems into equations. Those equations are the mathematical models for the real-life situations described by the word problems. Computers use mathematical models to analyse and study processes and problems in economics, business, weather forecasting, chemistry, physics, engineering and many other fields.

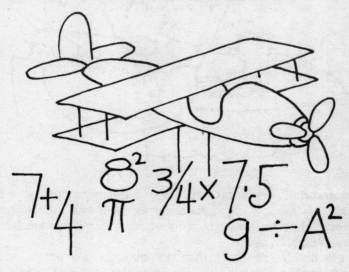

Memory The internal or main memory of the computer consists of rows of chips (integrated circuits) that store information as binary digits.

Think of memory as a series of mailboxes. At any given time, a box may or may not have mail (information) inside. An empty box is a 0; a box with mail is a 1.

External memories include tapes, disks, cassettes and other devices that store information as patterns of magnetized areas on a magnetic recording surface.

Memory map A diagram that shows how the main memory of a computer is laid out, what parts are used for what purposes.

Menu In a restaurant, a menu gives you a list of items from which to choose. You look at the list and select what you want to eat.

A computer menu gives you choices, too. The computer menu is a list of program functions, each labelled with a number or letter. To select a function, you press its number or letter on your keyboard. The computer then puts that particular sequence of instructions to work for you.

Microcomputer Technically speaking, a microcomputer is a digital computer that uses a microprocessor as its central processing unit. A microcomputer is made by connecting the microprocessor to a memory integrated circuit.

For practical purposes, a microcomputer is any small, desk-top computer designed to be used by one person at a time. The average microcomputer has about 100K of memory.

Microprocessor As the name implies, a microprocessor is an extremely small central processing unit (CPU). The microprocessor contains, on a small silicon chip, all the circuitry needed to perform the CPU's functions. Microprocessors are the 'brains' of all personal computers. And they are used in many other modern machines including calculators, microwave ovens, video games and certain automobiles.

Microsecond One millionth of a second. Today's high-speed computers can process a piece of information in as little as a millionth of a second. And some can even do it in a billionth of a second!

Microwave Radio and television signals are all transmitted as electromagnetic waves. Microwaves are electromagnetic waves with frequencies somewhere between infrared radiation and shortwave radio. These ultrahigh-frequency waves are used to transmit voices and information over data communications systems as well as to cook food in microwave ovens.

Mill Another name for the central processing unit of a computer.

Mill time The total time spent by the computer in processing one particular job. In a time-sharing system, the mill time taken for each user will be quite different from *real time*.

Minicomputer Smaller than a mainframe and larger than a microcomputer, the minicomputer is about the size of a record player. A mini can be used by several people at once, and is not too much more complicated than a micro. The typical mini has several hundred K (kilobytes) of memory and stores information on hard disks rather than floppy disks.

MIPS Stands for Million Instructions Per Second. A measure of the speed of a computer.

Mnemonic According to the *Oxford English Dictionary*, a mnemonic is something that is 'intended to aid the memory'.

In science classes, teachers often tell students to use mnemonic rhymes and verbal patterns to memorize the bones in the body, the nerves of the brain, or the planets of the solar system. One mnemonic to help students memorize the planets is '*M*artha *V*isits *E*very *M*onday *A*nd *J*ust *S*tays *U*ntil *N*oon *P*eriod' – for *M*ercury, *V*enus, *E*arth, *M*ars, *A*steroid belt, *J*upiter, *S*aturn, *U*ranus, *N*eptune and *P*luto.

94

In computer programming, mnemonics help programmers remember the meaning of an instruction or the name of a file of information. For example, MULT is easily remembered as the command for multiplication. And information in your school file might be given easy-to-remember labels such as ATT for attendance record, EXTRAC for extracurricular activities, and CORESCHED for course schedule.

Mode A manner or way of doing things; a method of operation. Some examples:
- A school looking for new teachers is in a hiring mode.
- A company trying to increase sales and build a new factory is in a growth mode.
- A person sitting at a keyboard terminal with a video display screen is programming in a conversational or interactive mode, while someone who writes his program on punched cards works in a batch mode.

Modem Short for MOdulator-DEModulator. A modem lets you link your home computer to other computers via the telephone line. To do this you need a modem at either end of the phone connection. The modem at your end translates the digital signals from the computer into a continuous form suitable for transmission over the telephone line. At the receiving end, a modem translates these signals back into the digital form that can be accepted by the recipient's computer.

Modular A modular system consists of many standard compatible component parts, or modules. You can change and expand a modular system by adding and rearranging the modules. A modular computer or other electronic system is easy to repair. If a part fails, just pull it out and plug in a modular replacement.

Modular computer programming techniques break programs into small, easy-to-write modules. Each module performs a particular function and can be treated as a separate program.

Monte Carlo A statistical technique involving random numbers (numbers you pick out of a hat, so to speak). Here's how it works.

Let's say I divide a bingo card into quarters and shade in one of the quarters. By playing bingo, I select locations on the card at random —

B1, G6, N4 and so on. After a while, the ratio of points picked inside the shaded area to the total points picked should be 1:4 – corresponding to the fact that the shaded area is ¼ of the total area of the card.

Monte Carlo wouldn't work well with a bingo card because there aren't enough points to choose from. For Monte Carlo to be accurate, thousands of trial points must be selected. While that makes Monte Carlo slow and inefficient for bingo, it does work with a high-speed computer that can pick a thousand points in a fraction of a second.

MOS Stands for Metal Oxide Semiconductor. A type of high-density integrated circuit.

Mother board A large printed circuit board supporting wiring patterns and edge-connectors. Many smaller printed circuit boards, including processing units, memories and interfaces, may be plugged into the mother board. (See also *printed circuit board*.)

Mouse A device for pointing to information on the screen, so that you can tell the computer what you want it to do. The mouse is a small shell with a wire attached that sits on the table top next to the terminal. As you move the mouse around on the table, the cursor moves on the screen accordingly.

Multiplexer A multiplexer is a machine that combines transmissions from several remote computer terminals and sends them over a single telephone line. With multiplexers, you save money because you need fewer phone lines in your data communications system.

Multiprocessing Any computer system with more than one central processing unit. One type of multiprocessing system links several small central processing units together to handle data processing. Another multiprocessing configuration has a few small processors feeding information to a large central processing unit that handles most of the information processing.

Multiprogramming In multiprogramming, the computer's main memory holds more than one program. The memory is divided into separate segments called partitions; each partition holds a program. The size and number of partitions can be varied to increase the efficiency of data processing.

Naive user A naive user is somebody who wants the computer to do something, but does not know much about how the computer works. Many business people, video game enthusiasts and home computer owners are naive users — they bought their machines to accomplish specific goals and don't care much about learning to program. On the other hand, computer professionals and many scientists, mathematicians, engineers and computer hobbyists are not naive users; they enjoy working with computers and learning how they function.

NAND Stands for NOT-AND. A logical operation that is the negative or reverse of AND. A *NAND gate* is an electronic circuit whose output in binary code is 0 only if all inputs are 1. This is the opposite of an *AND gate*, where the output is 1 only if all inputs are 1.

Nanosecond A billionth of a second. There are as many nanoseconds in a second as there are seconds in 30 years. Today's fastest mainframe computer can make a decision in a nanosecond, which means the computer can perform a billion or so mathematical and logical operations every second.

Network A system of interconnected computers, terminals and other devices.

Nibble A nibble is a piece of information half a byte, or four bits, long.

Node A junction point in a network, such as one of the computers in a network or a switching centre.

Noise An undesirable variation in the voltage, current or frequency of an electrical signal. Noise can cause a program to run incorrectly or fail completely. Causes include random electron motion, thunderstorms, power surges and nearby electrical machinery.

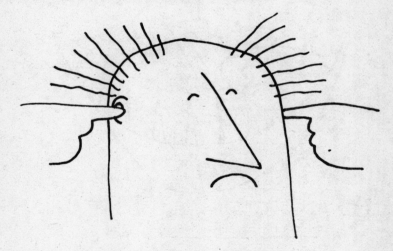

No-op (NOP) A no-op (no operation) instruction. A no-op is a written instruction that has absolutely no effect on the computer's operation. It is used to reserve space in a program for possible future additions. Using a no-op instruction is something like keeping a padlock on an empty locker you think you might need at some point in the future.

NOR Short for NOT-OR. A logical operation that is the negative or reverse of OR. A *NOR gate* is an electronic circuit whose output in binary code is 0 if any of the inputs is 1. This is the opposite of an *OR gate*, where the output is 1 if any of the inputs is 1.

NOT A logical operator with the condition that if statement X is true, then the statement NOT X is false. If X is false, then NOT X is true. A *NOT gate* is an electronic circuit whose output is 1 when its input is 0 and vice versa. (See also *inverter*.)

Number crunching Number crunching is using the computer to perform repetitive, routine arithmetic — addition, square roots, exponents and so forth. Because of their high speed, computers can crunch large quantities of numbers in a very short time.

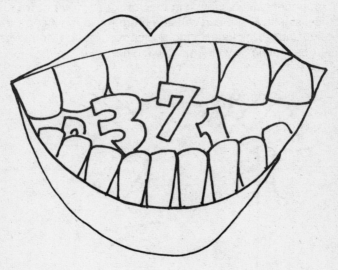

Object program A program in machine language — the binary code that computers understand. This is the program the computer actually executes.

OCR Stands for optical character recognition. Techniques for getting computers to read printed words, so that people do not have to type in large amounts of data on keyboards. This is difficult. Reading hand-printed or hand-written words is even more difficult, but progress is being made.

OEM Stands for Original Equipment Manufacturer. An OEM buys computers and other electronic components and builds them into its own products. A company that manufactures fighter planes, for example, might buy a computer from IBM or Honeywell and install it in the plane's on-board guidance system. The aeroplane manufacturer then sells the plane — along with the computer — to the R.A.F., a foreign government or one of its other customers.

In contrast with an OEM, an *end user* is any company that buys the computer for its own use and not for resale as a part of its products.

Off line A device not hooked up to the computer is said to be off line.

On line A device hooked up to the computer is said to be on line. On-line devices work in conjunction with the computer's central processing unit.

Op-cod Short for operation code. The instructions, in an electronic binary code pattern, that tell the computer circuits to perform some particular operation. For example, the code 111010101001 might instruct the computer to add two numbers together.

Open ended Open-ended computer systems are designed to expand in anticipation of future growth. Items can be added to such systems without changing those parts already in existence.

Operand Anything that is manipulated or operated on by the computer. An operand may be information, a variable, a number or an address in memory.
Consider the equation $A + B = C$. A and B are the operands, the plus sign (+) is the operator, and C is the result of the operation.

Operating system Special software that makes sure your computer performs smoothly and efficiently. The operating system sees to it that information flows through the system in an orderly fashion. It also keeps the computer from trying to do too many things at once, and makes sure there's enough unoccupied space in memory to store the results of programs the system is running.

Operation cycle The series of operations performed by a computer's central processing unit (CPU) for each instruction in a program. The steps in this cycle are:
1. Retrieve the next instruction from memory.
2. Put the instruction into the CPU.
3. Add a '1' to the program counter. The counter keeps track of which instruction is to be carried out next.
4. Find any additional information the computer may need to carry out the instruction.
5. Perform the task specified by the instruction.
6. Prepare to start the cycle over again.

Operators The people who enter information and instructions into the computer. They operate the machine and retrieve the results.

Optical disks Laser-optical video disks store information as microscopic areas of light and dark. A beam of light reads the information; no device comes in physical contact with the surface of the disk. As a result, video disks never wear out.

A single video disk can hold billions of bytes of information. One disadvantage of video disks is that once information is recorded, it can never be erased or re-recorded.

OR A logical operation that produces results depending on the pieces of information acted on. In an OR operation, the result is 1 if one or more of the bits operated on is 1. An *OR gate* is an electronic circuit whose output is 1 if any of the inputs is 1.

Output The information that is coming out of a computer. Compare this with *input*.

Overflow When you perform addition or multiplication and the result is too big for the machine to handle, an overflow occurs. Let's say you multiply 1,000,000,000 by 1,000,000,000 on a pocket calculator with a ten-digit read-out. Obviously, the result—1,000,000,000,000,000,000—is too large to display and an overflow condition will occur. Calculators and computers indicate overflow with a flashing display, warning light, alarm or other warning signal.

Overlay If a program is too large to fit into the computer's internal memory, the parts not being used are held in external storage. When they are needed, a special control program calls them into the main memory. This technique is known as overlay.

Package Software sold for a specific purpose, such as accounting or word processing, complete and ready for use.

Paddle A knob or other device connected to the computer, mainly to control games.

Paging On a video display screen, paging is switching from one page or screenful of information to the next. In memory, a page is a section of storage. To find a piece of information on that page, you need to specify both a page number (or page address) and an address that pinpoints the item within the page.

Paper tape Rolls of punched paper tape are a low-cost — if old-fashioned — medium for storing information.

The tape is punched with sprocket holes that allow the roll to be fed through a mechanical reader. Paper tape can input information to the computer at the rather rapid rate of 1,000 characters per second.

A character is recorded as a row of holes punched across the width of the tape. The punch pattern corresponds to the bit pattern (a series of 1s and 0s) in a binary-code character. Most tape systems have 8-position punch patterns that can represent the 128 alphanumeric characters and symbols, with one parity bit.

Paper tapes are compact, inexpensive, easy to carry and fast-reading. However, they obviously can't be erased and paper can be easily damaged.

Parallel In parallel operation, data is transmitted several bits (pieces of information) at a time. This contrasts with serial operation, in which data is transmitted one bit at a time.

Pretend each bit of data is a musical note. Playing a chord on a piano is a parallel operation, because several notes or bits are transmitted to the ear simultaneously. But playing a tune on a clarinet is a serial operation, since wind instruments can be played only one note at a time.

Parallel transmission is naturally faster than serial. But it is also more expensive because it requires additional circuitry to transmit multiple bits.

In the computer, parallel operation lets you transmit or process a byte, word, record, or other unit of information composed of many bits as a single unit of data.

Parameter   A variable quantity in a program that can be given different values by the user or by data-collecting instruments.

Parity check   A way of checking whether a mistake has been made by the electronics in storing or transmitting a binary number. An extra bit is added to each number and set to a 1 or a 0 so that there is always an even number of bits in each byte. Then the character can be checked later, and if a bit has been lost or gained inadvertently, the number of bits will be odd, not even, warning the system that a mistake has been made. Of course, there is no way of knowing what the correct character should have been, but at least a request can be made for that character to be sent again. Sometimes odd parity rather than even is used.

Partition sort   A rapid sorting technique used by the computer to divide a number of items into groups or subsets.

Say we have 30 children's blocks, each one a different size. Pick one at random and call it 'A'. Put all blocks smaller than A in one pile, and all blocks larger than A in a second pile. You have just sorted the pile of blocks into two piles grouped by size – larger than A and smaller than A. This is how a partition sort works.

A partition sort is faster than a bubble sort and is much more efficient for sorting a large number of items. (See also *bubble sort.*)

Pascal   An educational computer language used to teach students about programming and the elements of computer science. Pascal is designed to encourage students to form good programming habits and it is fairly easy to learn.

Pascal, Blaise   (1623–1662)   As a teenager, this French mathematician and inventor built the world's first practical calculator. Pascal's adding machine consisted of a set of interlocking cogs and wheels

105

mounted on various axles. Pascal constructed the device to help his father do tax computations.

Password   A secret code that gives you access to a computer system. Each user has his or her own special password. Passwords prevent unauthorized people from using the system.

Patch   If you rip your jeans, you could repair them with a patch — a small piece of material attached to the trousers to cover the damaged area. Well, computer programs can be patched, too.

If a program contains an error or weakness, a small set of instructions known as a patch can be written in to correct the deficiency. When too many patches are holding the program together, it is time to sit down and rewrite it entirely.

Peek   A function in BASIC that allows you to read the contents of a location in memory directly, circumventing BASIC's own ways of storing numbers.

Peripherals   All the accessories that can be hooked up to your computer. Peripheral devices include cassette tape recorders, floppy disk drives, printers, joy sticks, modems, terminals, keyboards, plotters and light pens. Such devices increase the computing power and flexibility of your system by helping it process and transmit information as quickly and efficiently as possible.

PERT   Stands for Program Evaluation and Review Technique. Also known as *critical path analysis*. Let's say a factory, an accounting firm, a college or a research laboratory needs to run some special projects on the computer. Their system is nearly always in demand, so they must set up a timetable for completing these projects. The timetable spells out the events that must take place in order to complete the project, and what resources must be dedicated to making these events occur. This planning technique is called PERT.

Ping-pong   A programming technique for processing files of information stored on more than one magnetic tape reel.
   This technique uses two magnetic tape drives. While one processes a reel, the other sits idle, ready to go to work on a fresh reel.
   When a reel is processed, the computer switches to the drive with a fresh reel of tape. The old tape is taken off the other drive and a fresh reel put into place. In this way, the computer jumps back and forth between the two tape drives like a ping-pong ball until the entire file is processed.

Pipelining   In the pipelining technique, a computer prepares to receive its next instruction while it is still working on its current instruction. Pipelining greatly increases the processing speed of the system.

Plotter   A device that lets the computer draw pictures, diagrams, patterns, symbols, graphs and designs with a pen held in a mechanical arm. Plotters can produce drawings much faster than artists or draughtsmen can.

Plug board Also known as a *patch board* or *jack panel*. A device used to control the functions of certain types of computers. Various devices and connections are plugged into sockets on the back of the board. You can select functions for the computer to perform by changing the interconnections on the board.

Pneumatic computer A computer that stores and transmits information by means of the flow rate or pressure of a gas or a liquid.

Point-of-sale (POS) terminal A computer terminal that looks and works like a cash register. The POS terminal records transactions; calculates totals, subtotals, and VAT; and prints out an itemized receipt. A record of all purchases is transmitted from the terminal to the store's central computer. Information from POS terminals helps the computer keep track of sales and inventory.

Poke A command in BASIC that lets you store data into memory locations directly, as with the function *peek*, rather than using BASIC's way of storing numbers.

Polish notation A special notation that lets pocket calculators and computers do arithmetic more efficiently. In Polish notation, equations are read from right to left. The expression A+B would be written as +AB, which, read from right to left, means, 'Take B, take A, and add them together.' This notation was named 'Polish notation' because no one could pronounce the name of its Polish inventor, Jan Lukasiewicz.

Poll Let's say the computer is linked to multiple remote terminals via several communications channels. The computer regularly polls or tests each channel, and connects when it finds one that is either free for transmission or is sending a message to the computer. Polling prevents all of the terminals from trying to talk with the computer at the same time.
　Polling is much like trying to call up five different friends over the phone. Some of the lines may be engaged. When one is free, the phone rings at the other end, the receiver is picked up, and you can begin to talk with the person at the other end.

Ports Ports are outlets where printers, storage devices, terminals and other peripheral equipment can plug into the computer. The greater the number of ports, the more flexible the computer system.

108

Post-mortem Television's Quincy is an expert in post-mortem (after death) examinations, known to the medical world as autopsies.

In the computer world, a post-mortem routine is used to provide information about a program after the program has finished running. And just as the coroner's examination can reveal much about the cause of death, the computer's post-mortem examination is useful for pointing out errors and other problems that may be present in the program.

Prestel British Telecom's *viewdata* service.

Printed circuit board (PCB) Also known as *printed circuit card*. The PCB is a thin insulating board. Integrated circuits, resistors, capacitors and other electronic components are mounted on the board and interconnected as a circuit by a pattern of conductive lines etched on to the board's surface. This etched circuit pattern eliminates the need to connect components with wire.

Printer A typewriterlike device controlled by a computer. The printer prints results of programs, information retrieved from memory, and other computer output on either individual sheets or continuous strips of paper.

There are two basic types of printers:

● Impact printers print by striking a typing element against the paper through a carbon or inked ribbon. Typewriters are impact printers.

● Nonimpact printers print by applying heat, light or electricity to specially treated papers – similar to the way a photocopy machine makes reproductions. They can also spray the ink on to the paper in a jet.

Print-out Paper documents that have come from a computer printer.

Probability Probability measures the odds of a given event taking place. For example, if you flip a coin, the probability is one out of two that it will show heads, and one out of two that it will show tails.

In a strictly mathematical sense, probability is defined as the number of ways an event can happen divided by the number of possible happenings. The coin toss can result in only a single happening (either it shows heads or it shows tails), but the number of possible happenings is two: heads and tails. Thus, the probability of tossing heads is one divided by two, or one out of two.

Calculating the probabilities of more complex events can be a long, tedious process. And that's where the computer's high-speed data processing capabilities can help.

Procedure In some programming languages, another name for a *subroutine*.

Process control The use of a dedicated computer to control something, such as a machine in a factory or a scientific experiment.

Processor Another name for *central processing unit*.

Program The sequence of instructions written to make the computer carry out a specific task. The program tells the computer what to do and how to do it. *Applications programs* tell the computer how to solve a specific problem, while *systems programs* control the internal operation of the computer system. Program in this meaning is always spelt the American way, without an -me.

Program counter A register in the computer that keeps track of the next instruction to be executed. It holds the address of that instruction, and every time the computer completes an instruction it adds 1 to the program counter.

110

Programmer A person who writes computer programs.

PROM Stands for Programmable Read-Only Memory. Ordinary ROMs have their information loaded into them at the factory. The user himself, though, can put information into a PROM, using a special machine called (would you believe) a 'PROM-zapper'. The information is held in thousands of fusable links that are either burnt through or not – data once stored in a PROM cannot be erased, but see EPROM.

Protocols The rules by which computers exchange information on a network in such a way that different machines can understand each other.

Punch card Computer information may be stored on a series of punched paper cards. Each card is about 7½ inches by 3¼ inches and is 80 rows wide by 12 rows high, for a total of 960 locations where holes may be punched. The pattern of punched holes corresponds to coding information in binary form. (See also *Hollerith, Herman.*)

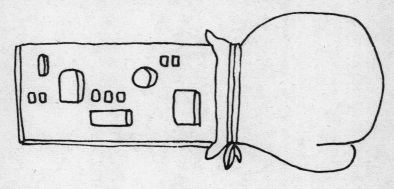

Queue A queue is the waiting line at a ticket window. In data processing, a queue is a line of programs waiting to be run by the computer, or a *FIFO*. And in data communications, message queueing is a system in which a central computer stores messages from several remote terminals until they have been processed, and then routes each message to its destination.

QWERTY The layout of the normal typewriter keyboard, so called after the first letters in the top row of keys QWERTYUIOP. Most computers also use QWERTY, even though it is very hard to use.

RAM A RAM is not a sheep; it is the memory the computer uses to carry out the instructions you give it. When you load a program into the computer, it is stored in RAM.

RAM stands for Random-Access Memory. Random access means you can go straight to the location in the memory you seek without having to seach through the entire contents of the memory in sequence.

RAM is a read-write memory: you can read (retrieve information) from or write (input information) to the RAM.

RAM is a 'volatile' memory – all the information stored in RAM is lost when the power is turned off.

RAMPS Stands for Resource Allocation in Multi-Project Schedule. Any part of the total computer system – the machinery, the programs, the people who operate it – can be considered a resource. Large organizations use RAMPS to allocate their resources in the most efficient way possible.

Raster scan   The way a television, and most computer screens, constructs its pictures, as a series of horizontal lines (625 in British television, repeated 25 times a second). Other, rarer, computer screens make pictures out of dots put anywhere on the screen in any order.

Raw data   Information waiting to be processed by the computer.

Read   To retrieve information from a computer memory. The act of reading does not alter the information in any way.

Read-write memory A type of computer memory in which the contents can be erased and changed. RAM, magnetic tapes and floppy disks are all examples of read-write memory.

Real numbers Numbers which include decimal fractions (4·210036, 3807·56) as opposed to *integers* (4, 1997). It is important to remember that, held in a computer, real numbers are never absolutely exact. Most computers give you nine *significant digits* at least, which is usually plenty, but problems can arise – see *accuracy*.

Real-time A real-time computer system can think and act as fast as the actual process it is measuring or simulating. For example, the computer that controls the gun in a tank must work in real-time; otherwise, the enemy will be long gone by the time the gun is aimed and fired.

Record A part of a file that contains all the information about one particular thing. For instance in a school file, one record might contain all the information about one pupil. Different *fields* within the file would contain his name, address, date of birth, form, etc.

Recording density The density of magnetized spots (each representing a single piece of information or 'bit') on the surface of magnetic storage media such as tapes, disks and drums. On magnetic tapes, recording densities of 256 or 512 bits per inch is common. The rate at which you can record data on the tape depends on the recording density and the speed of the tape drive.

Register A portion of memory used to store information and instructions currently being processed by the control unit or the arithmetic/logic unit of the computer's central processing unit (CPU). Registers are physically located in the CPU.

Report A printed analysis of information produced by the computer. To get the computer to produce a report, you need a report program that specifies the format and content of the report you'd like to see.

Resident Any program permanently stored in the main memory of the computer. Some resident programs include:
- The editor, a program designed to handle text.
- The assembler, a program that converts programming language into binary code.
- The debugger, a program that helps you find software errors.

Return-to-reference recording A technique for storing information in magnetic memory media such as disks, drums and tapes. Each spot on the magnetic surface can be magnetized above the existing or reference level of magnetization in the medium to represent the binary digit '1'. By applying a pulse of energy, you can change the level of magnetization of any spot from 0 to 1; a second pulse changes it back to 0.

RF (radio frequency) modulator A device that converts computer output signals to radio frequency signals that can be fed into a standard television set. RF modulators let you play video games on your colour television.

Ring A form of *local area network* in which the wire actually connects all the devices together in a closed ring, so all messages come back to where they started from. The sending device can then check them to see whether they have been received.

Robot The idea of an artificial human being, a mechanical device that can walk about, see things, handle things, understand our speech and talk to us. Despite all that has been said about robots, nothing remotely like one has ever been built, and we do not know if one ever will,

because the technical problems are enormous. However, there are machines in factories now that are commonly called robots. They do not look remotely like people: they are basically long mechanical arms that can put parts together and weld and paint things. The word robot comes from the 1921 play *R.U.R.* (for Rossum's Universal Robots), by the Czech dramatist Karel Čapek.

Roll in, roll out To roll in is to carry out a process in the computer by bringing parts of the process into main memory in sequence. To roll out is to remove a process from main memory. This technique is used when the computer has to shift quickly from one process to another.

Roll on Information not needed by the computer to perform its everyday operations is usually stored on tape or disks that can be kept in a cabinet or on a shelf. When the information is required for processing, the reel is located, taken out of the cabinet, put on a tape drive and transferred to another tape on a second tape drive that is plugged directly into the computer for on-line use. This technique is called a roll on.

ROM Stands for Read-Only Memory. The computer's programming language and start-up routines are stored in ROM. These are the built-in operating instructions used by the computer. Without ROM, you'd have to reload the computer every time you turned it on.

ROM is called a read-only memory because you can read (retrieve information) from ROM, but you can't put information into ROM. The input for ROM is permanently set at the factory.

ROM is a 'nonvolatile' memory, which means the information stored in ROM cannot be erased, changed or lost even if the power is turned off.

Rotate A computer instruction that causes the 'bits' in a word to shift a certain number of places to the left or to the right. If a word is shifted to the right, for example, the bits at the right end of the word get pushed off and reappear at the other end:

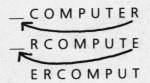

Rotating the word 'computer' two places to the right produces the word 'ercomput'.

Routine A set of instructions that forms a part of a computer program. Routines instruct the computer to carry out specific functions and tasks.

Run To begin the execution of a computer program.

Scale Let's say you want to multiply two numbers, but they're too big for the computer to handle. You can divide both numbers by a common scale factor to scale them down to a size acceptable to the computer. Then, after the multiplication is performed, you multiply the result by the scale factor to scale it back up to its true value.

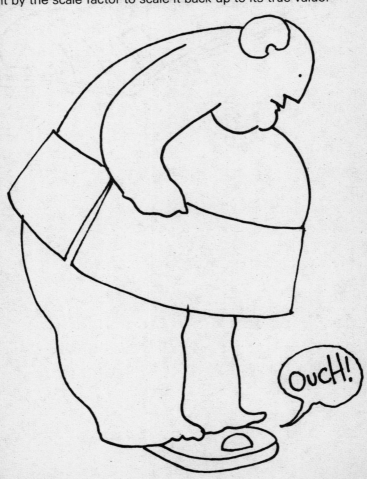

Scratch pad memory A small, fast auxiliary memory used for temporary information storage. Scratch pad memories help increase the overall data processing speed of the computer system because they're faster than the computer's main memory.

Scrolling Moving text up and down on a screen; sometimes also moving it from side to side. A common feature of word processors.

Security Any measures taken to prevent damage, theft or unauthorized access to a computer system or the information held on it.

Selection sort A simple sorting technique used to put the items of a small file in order. Here's how selection sorting works.

Assume we have a list of numbers:

2
3
1

Go down the list, look for the smallest number, and exchange it with the first number in the list:

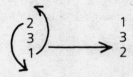

Now, repeat the procedure. Start with the second number in the list, since the first is already the smallest. Find the second smallest number, and exchange it with the second number in the list:

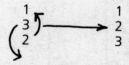

Repeat the procedure until the list is in ascending order, with the smallest number on top and the largest at the bottom:

1
2
3

Semiconductor The crystalline substance used to make chips and transistors – the circuits in computers.

Silicon is the material most often used as a semiconductor. Silicon is also the main ingredient of ordinary beach sand and it is one of the most plentiful elements on Earth.

The silicon used in chips is grown in a laboratory. It is 99·9 per cent pure. By adding slight chemical impurities to the silicon, scientists are able to change its electrical characteristics. Silicon crystals used in semiconductors are sliced into wafers as thin as this page and cut into tiny chips smaller than a halfpenny.

At room temperature, the semiconductor's capacity to conduct electric current lies somewhere between a conductor (like copper wire) and an insulator (like rubber).

Sentinel A group of 'bits' that indicates a specific condition such as the end of a reel of tape or the end of a record.

Sequential access The method used to find a piece of information stored on magnetic tape. In sequential access, you must run through the tape in sequence before you reach the information you seek. This is the way tape cassettes work. You have to use 'rewind' or 'fast forward' to get to a song in the middle of the tape.

Serial A technique for handling information in sequence, one bit at a time. (See also *parallel*.)

Shift A computer instruction that causes bits in a word to shift to the left or to the right. When the word shifts, the bits on the end drop off and are lost. The empty space at the other end is filled with zeros.

1 0 1 1 1	Shift two places to the right.
_ _ 1 0 1 ↘ ↘	The two digits at right drop off and are
1 1	lost. Two empty spaces open up at left.
0 0 1 0 1	Zeros fill the empty spaces.

Significant digits In a number, the digits whose values are known to be accurate. The number 123·4 has four significant digits. The number 678,000 has three significant digits if it is accurate to the nearest thousand.

Silicon Valley An area in the Santa Clara Valley of California famous as the home of more semiconductor manufacturers and other high-tech electronics companies than anywhere else in the world. The Valley takes its name from silicon, the principal ingredient of semiconductor chips.

Simplex A data communications line or device that allows transmission in one direction only. Radios and televisions are simplex devices — they can receive but they can't send.

Simulator A program that simulates the behaviour of an aeroplane, a spaceship, radar or other real-life device. Simulators provide a safe means for training people to operate such machines that are normally operated in potentially dangerous situations.

Slave A device under the control of another device. Or, a device that imitates the operation of another device. (See also *master/slave system*.)

Slow death The gradual deterioration and failure of an integrated circuit, resistor or other device.

Smalltalk A programming language developed by Xerox.

Smoke test A test in which new equipment is turned on for the first time to see if it will work. If there's a short circuit in the components, the machine may 'go up in smoke'.

Software Computer programs – the instructions that tell the computer what to do. Software is available on cassette tape, disk and plug-in cartridges. You can choose from thousands of different programs written to be used with personal computers.

Software-compatible If two computers are software-compatible, the software designed for one will also work with the second computer. Software-compatible computers speak the same machine language.

Software documentation Instruction manuals that tell programmers, operators and users what a program does, how it is written and how to use it.

Solid-state Refers to electronic circuits and components made from silicon, germanium and other solid substances, as opposed to valves, which contain gas. Common solid-state devices include transistors, diodes and resistors.

Sort To arrange a group of items according to size, number, alphabetical order, or some other organizational scheme. Computer sorting techniques include *bubble sorts, partition sorts* and *selection sorts*.

SOS To computer manufacturers, this well-known Morse code warning stands for Silicon On Sapphire – an integrated circuit in which a layer of sapphire increases the speed of operation.

Source program Programs written in assembly language or high-level language. Computers translate source programs into object programs (programs written in machine language) before carrying them out. In this way, source programs do indeed serve as the source for all programs run by the computer.

Speech recognition Ways of making computers understand human speech, picked up by a microphone. Speech recognition is very difficult, but several systems exist now that can understand a few hundred different words. They have to be 'trained' with the voice of the person whom they are intended to understand. There are even some crude speech-recognition devices for home computers.

Spooling Spool stands for Simultaneous Peripheral Output On Line and refers to the computer's ability to process information while controlling input and output devices such as tape drives, card readers, keyboards and video display screens. The spooling technique ensures that the computer is not held back from working at full speed by these slower peripheral machines.

Spreadsheet program A program for handling a businessman's accounts and helping him plan projected sales, profits and losses and the like.

Stack A region of memory that works something like a stack of papers in an office in-tray.

First you place a word in the stack (represented as a sheet of paper and an in-tray in the drawing below).

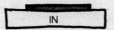

As you add words to the stack, that first item gets buried beneath them.

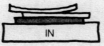

When you want to retrieve information from the stack, the computer has to take the top sheet off the pile. So, the last word you put on the stack is the first word you must take out.

You are not allowed to remove words from the bottom or the middle of the stack.

To reach the first item you put into the stack, you must remove items from the top one at a time until you reach the bottom of the pile.

In computer jargon, piling a word on a stack is a 'push'. Removing a word is a 'pull' or 'pop'.

Stacks simplify certain operations. They're often used as a temporary storage or buffer between a fast device and a slow device. (See also *LIFO*.)

Stand-alone   Stand-alone devices are self-contained machines. A stand-alone can operate by itself, with no add-on devices or outside support.

Stanford mouse   A computer input device that looks like a mouse on roller skates. Rolling the plastic mouse on a table top controls the movement of the cursor on the video display screen.

Static memory   Computer memory that, unlike *dynamic memory*, does not have to be refreshed – it holds its contents just so long as the power is on. It uses *flip-flop* circuits to store the data instead of capacitors and is more expensive than dynamic RAM.

Store   A memory device or medium. A store can receive information, hold it for as long as you like, and allow you to retrieve the information whenever you need it. *To store* means to place information in a memory device.

String   A series of characters (GOOD MORNING STARSHINE) as opposed to a number (765·2340551). Of course you can have figures in a string (GET YOUR KICKS ON ROUTE 66) but the computer will not be able to perform arithmetic on them.

Subroutine   Often there are several different places in a program where the same sequence of operations has to be carried out. It would be wasteful of time and memory to write out all the instructions into the program each time, so programmers use *subroutines*. These are parts of a program to which the computer can branch when required, and at the end of the subroutine the computer goes *back to where it came from* in the main program. There has to be a special facility in the computer hardware for remembering where it came from. Computers often have libraries of useful subroutines which can be added to programs when needed.

Successive approximation   A trial-and-error technique used to solve equations. In successive approximation, the computer guesses the solution to an equation. Based on the result, it decides whether the next guess should be higher or lower. The process is repeated until the computer comes up with a guess that, for practical purposes, is close to the exact solution.

Swap   Some programs are too large to fit in the computer's internal memory. So, only a part of the program is kept in the computer; the rest is held in external storage (tape or disk).

Let's say you need to call on a part of the program in external storage. There's not enough room in memory to accommodate more information. And so you make a swap, exchanging the part of the program on tape with the portion in memory. Swapping isn't efficient, but it does let you get along with a limited amount of internal memory.

Synchronous   See *asynchronous.*

Syntax   Your English teacher will tell you that syntax is a set of rules governing the way in which words are put together to form phrases and sentences. But to computer programmers, syntax is the set of rules that dictates how commands in programming languages fit together to form statements and instructions.

Systems analyst   The person who puts computer systems together. The systems analyst determines the combination of hardware and software best suited to solving the user's problems.

Systems software   Systems programs: see *program.*

Table A grid of information stored in memory. Tables consist of horizontal rows and vertical columns. An individual item in the table may be located by specifying its position in the table. Or, you can specify its key (an identifying label of digits). *Table look-up* is the process of searching a table to find items belonging to a particular key.

Tablet A small board attached to a computer and used for drawing pictures. As you move a stylus around on the tablet, the cursor on the computer screen moves accordingly.

Tag In a clothing store, a tag is a paper label attached to a garment to identify its size and price. In the computer, a tag is a collection of digits or characters attached to a record of information as an identifying label. The difference between a tag and a key is that the key is not actually attached to the record.

Telecommunications Any system in which electric or electromagnetic signals transmit information between two or more separate locations. Telecommunications systems link computers to each other and to remote computer terminals.

Teletex A particular form of *electronic mail* used in offices, with special terminals like word processors. Teletex is rather like a fancy Telex system.

Teletext (Different from teletex!) A form of *videotex* in which information is broadcast along with ordinary television programmes and picked up by specially-adapted TV sets. The B.B.C.'s teletext service is called Ceefax and I.T.V.'s is called Oracle; from these you can get news summaries, the weather forecast, programme details, and subtitles for the deaf. Unlike *viewdata*, however, it is only one-way; you cannot feed information back into the computer from your home.

Teletypewriter A machine consisting of a keyboard and a printer in a single unit. Also known as *teleprinter*.

Terminal A terminal consists of a keyboard and a video display in a single unit. The keyboard sends information to the computer; the video screen displays computer output. There are two types of computer terminals:

- A 'dumb terminal' does not contain any computer circuitry. It can communicate with the computer, but it can't perform data processing operations on its own.
- A 'smart terminal' can perform limited computer operations by itself because it contains some built-in computer circuitry. However, its primary function is to communicate with a regular computer.

Test bed   A collection of computer programs used in testing other programs.

Thermal printer   See *printer*.

Thin-film memory   An extremely fast, extremely compact type of magnetic storage medium. To construct such a memory, a layer of magnetic substance only a few millionths of an inch thick is deposited on a plate of glass or other nonmagnetic material. Then, microscopic areas on the film are polarized (electrically charged) to store digital information. A single binary digit can be retrieved from thin-film memory in about a billionth of a second.

Throughput A measure of the efficiency or speed of a computer. The throughput is defined as the number of instructions executed per second.

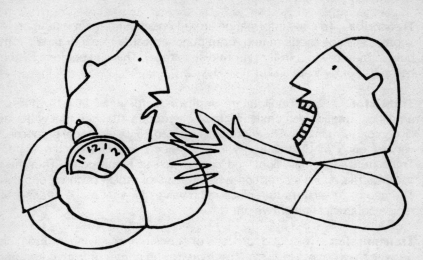

Time sharing A method of computer operation that allows two or more people to use the same computer at the same time. The computer shifts from terminal to terminal so rapidly that each user feels that he is alone with the computer. Time sharing lets you receive immediate responses to your questions and commands. And if there's an error in your program, you can change it right on the spot. For individual users, time sharing is much more efficient and enjoyable than batch processing.

Top-down approach An approach to programming in which you write the main segment of the program first and then work your way down to the smaller, less important segments. This is the way students write theses or long essays — they complete the body of the report first, and then they write the bibliography, introduction, title page, table of contents and other smaller sections.

Tracing An operating mode in which the computer displays each instruction on the screen or the printer as it executes it. This is very useful for finding mistakes in programs, but it slows down the computer a great deal.

Transaction processing   Using a computer to handle individual trans-actions with people on-line, for example, airline reservations or building society deposits and withdrawals.'

Transcribe   To copy information stored on one storage medium on to another storage medium (e.g. from punched cards to paper tape; from bubble memory to thin-film; from disk to tape). This can be done by the computer or by a special off-line device.

Transistor   A small solid-state semiconductor used as a switch or amplifier. Transistors consist of three electrodes attached to a wafer of silicon or germanium. The material is treated so its electrical properties vary at each of the places where an electrode touches the wafer. Transistors are small, light and can switch at high speed. They first came to the public's attention when transistor radios became popular. The use of transistors to replace radio valves is what makes transistor radios so small and lightweight.

Transmission   The act or process of sending or receiving information between two points (e.g. from memory to line printer or from computer to telephone line). There are two basic methods of transmitting information in electronic data processing systems:

● Synchronous transmission – transmits information at regular, precisely controlled time intervals.

● Asynchronous transmission – no timed pulses present; information is transmitted at irregular intervals.

Transparent   Anything you can see through as if it weren't there. In a data processing sense, a transparent event is something that occurs so quickly that the user never knows it happened.

Trap   A trap is an unusual condition detected by the computer while the program is running. For example, the program may call for an operation that, if carried out, will produce a result too big for the computer to handle. When the computer sees a trap, it prints a warning message notifying the operator of the cause of the problem.

Trouble-shooting People who hate machines might see trouble-shooting as blasting the computer with a shotgun at the first sign of trouble. In truth, trouble-shooting is a search for errors in a program or mechanical failures in the hardware. The trouble-shooter's job is to identify and eliminate the problem.

Turing, Alan (1912–1954) An English mathematician who contributed greatly to the development of the modern computer. Turing wrote a famous paper describing the Turing Machine, a theoretical computer, and showed that it could solve an unlimited variety of problems. He also helped develop the code-breaking computer Colossus.

Turing test Some day we may have computers which could be described as 'intelligent'. To solve arguments about whether a machine really was intelligent, Alan Turing suggested this test. You sit a friend in a room with a computer terminal. You tell him that at the other end of the terminal line is either a computer or another person. You invite your friend to have a conversation over the terminal. If after a time he cannot tell whether he is conversing with a person or a computer, then the computer can be called 'intelligent'.

Turnaround time   The time required to complete any given task. In data processing, turnaround time is the time it takes the computer to answer a question or run a program.

Turnkey system   Any system that is complete and ready to use. A turnkey computer system includes a main processor, an input device, an output device and software.

Turtle graphics   A method of drawing pictures on the computer screen by moving a turtle — a cursor (electronic blip) in the shape of a triangle. Some turtles are actually little carts that the computer can move around on the floor to draw lines with a pen. (See also *Logo*.)

Unbundling Selling computer hardware and software separately.

Univac I Built in 1951, Univac I was the first commercially successful computer system. Univac was also the first computer to use magnetic tape for input.

Universal Product Code (UPC) A mark found on many product packages, the UPC consists of an area of white with a combination of black bars of varying thicknesses.

An optical scanner built into the store's check-out counter reads the code and automatically rings the item up on the cash register. (See also *point-of-sale terminal*.)

Up A computer that is working properly. A programmer might say, 'I can't run my program until the computer goes up at 9 a.m. tomorrow.'

User-friendly Anybody who uses a computer is a user. User-friendly means the computer system is easy to use. User-friendly systems check errors, display information in easy-to-read formats and tell the user what he should do next.

Utility program Any program that helps the computer carry out its day-to-day activities, such as sorting files or transferring information from one device to another.

Validation Users frequently make mistakes in typing information into a computer, and the computer has no way of telling that the information is wrong. However, it can tell if the information is *ridiculously* wrong. For instance, if you had a program to work out the average age of a group of people, and one person was entered as being 2,000 years old, a *validity check* in the program could trap this and say, '*Wait* a minute!' You could include instructions in the program to reject any age over (say) 110 years. This is called validation.

Variable Any symbol representing a quantity that can change its value. In the equation $Y = X + 5$, Y and X are variables, while 5 is a constant that does not change value. If you assign a value of 12 to X, then Y takes on the value 17 (12+5). If $X = 2$, then $Y = 7$.

VDU Stands for Visual Display Unit or Video Display Unit. (See *video monitor*.)

Verification A way of trapping errors in computer input by having all the data typed twice. Whenever the second pass does not match the first, the machine stops, and the operator has to check carefully to see which is correct.

Video monitor A television set or other special TV screen for displaying computer input and output. A terminal is a video monitor combined with a keyboard. Video monitors are also known as *video display tubes* or *units*.

Videotex A general name for computer systems that enable you to receive information in your home on a modified television set. The information appears as words and sometimes crude pictures on the TV screen, but you must either have a special set or a converter box that plugs into an ordinary set. There are two kinds of videotex: *teletext* and *viewdata*.

Viewdata A videotex system that links your home TV set to a central computer over the ordinary telephone line. By keying in numbers on a control box you can get news, weather forecasts, train times, theatre information, jokes, advertisements and much more. You can even order goods from shops and book holidays over the system.

Virgin medium Any computer storage medium totally devoid of information – a paper tape with no holes, a bubble memory with no changes, a magnetic tape with no magnetized areas.

Virtual storage A clever feature of some computer operating systems that enables you to run a program that would normally be too big to fit in the machine's main memory. The operating system swaps parts of the program on and off disks as required. This is obviously much slower than if the main memory were big enough, but it means that the programmer does not have to rewrite the program.

VisiCalc® An easy-to-use package of *spreadsheet* programs marketed by Personal Software. VisiCalc® displays information on the screen as an electronic sheet or grid. Locations within the grid are treated as variables. To manipulate a variable, you apply an equation or logical operator to the variable's location in the grid.

VITAL Stands for Virtual Image Take-Off And Landing. VITAL is a computerized pilot training system that uses a video monitor to simulate flying. The program causes the simulator to react just as a real aeroplane would under actual operating conditions. With VITAL, a pilot-in-training can land in a blizzard or fly above a hurricane without ever setting foot in a real cockpit.

VLSI Stands for Very Large Scale Integration. Chips with even more component parts than *LSI*.

Voice synthesizer Remember how the computer aboard the U.S.S. *Enterprise* used to talk back to Captain Kirk in a stiff, robotlike voice? Well, thanks to the voice synthesizer, real-life computers can do that, too.

A voice synthesizer is an electronic circuit that simulates the human voice. It does not just play back a prerecorded actor's voice, but actually forms words by combining 100 different tones into patterns that make

up spoken English. Voice synthesizers are used to give the power of speech to computers, video games, clocks, hand-held language translators and pocket calculators.

Volatile   A volatile computer memory loses its store of information when the power is turned off; RAM is a volatile memory. *Nonvolatile* memories do not lose their contents when the power is turned off; cores, tapes, disks and cassettes are nonvolatile memories.

Von Neumann, John   (1903–1957)   John von Neumann originated the concept of a stored program: the idea that instructions can be represented as numbers and stored internally in the computer. Stored programs give computers the flexibility they need to perform many different tasks.

Williams tube storage   Traditionally, cathode ray tubes are used to display computer output. But F. C. Williams of the University of Manchester invented a modified cathode ray tube to store information as an energized portion of the tube's surface. His invention is known as the Williams tube.

Winchester disk   A kind of non-removable hard disk.

Word   The amount of information that the computer transfers into and out of memory at a time. The length of a word varies from one model of computer to another. Home computers tend to have 8-bit words, while larger machines have 16, 24, 32, or even 60-bit words.

Word processor   A computer functioning as an electronic typewriter with a built-in memory. Word processing speeds up preparation of text, stores documents and mailing lists, and eliminates the need to retype a page when a change is made.

Write   To store information in a computer memory.

X-Y plotter A computer output device which draws lines and points on a sheet of paper. The X-Y plotter is particularly useful for displaying output in the form of graphs. (See also *plotter.*)

Yield When a manufacturer produces chips from a wafer of silicon, some fraction of the chips will be defective. The yield is the percentage of good chips in a given batch.

Z

Zero suppression Before a computer prints out a number, it usually gets rid of unneeded zeros for the sake of readability. Thus, 345·3000 would be printed as 345·3, and 0087 would appear as 87.

Zuse, Konrad (1910–) A German engineer who designed and built the first working program-controlled computing machine. Zuse's machine was the first computer to use binary code rather than decimal numbering to store and manipulate information.